A Kid's Pocket Guide

ALL ABOUT ME IN D.C.

I would like to dedicate this book to the students at Bannockburn, Thomas W. Pyle and St. Bartholomew schools, and to all the families and kids (Coulter, Harrison, Chase, Pat, Peter, Pablo, Molly, Carly, Ethan, Liam, Annabelle, Marina, Dylan, Shannon, Madison, Davis, Lucas, Leah, Avery, Elliott, Brendan, Ari and Nick) who helped and went on my many field trips to D.C. I saw the city through your eyes. Thank you also to my wonderful editor Christine LePorte, the talented Chip Gestiehr, and all the curators, education departments, museum staff and rangers.

Corkey Hay DeSimone

www.AllAboutMEinDC.com

An Interactive Guide

20 Top Sights & Over 250 Fun Facts

How to use Your book

This is your book. YOU make the rules, but to get started here are some ideas:

Read cover to cover or pick a sight
Learn all about D.C., and surf our website.

Take the D.C. Challenge
Check out page 17.

Learn Fun Facts, Myths and More.
The more you know before you go, the better your trip will be.

Do Fave Fives and Personal Polls.
Keep track of your favorites. Poll your friends, teachers and family.

Doodle, Draw and Write.
Carry your book with you. Use it as your own personal time capsule.

On Our Website
Learn more, build your itinerary, and upload your photos on Flickr. LInk to our free app, games, Facebook page, Twitter posts and enewsletters.

www.AllAboutMEinDC.com

Table of Contents

My D.C.

Smithsonian

We the People

Monuments

Museums and More

If I could meet anyone in D.C. it would be.

- ☐ The President
- ☐ My Senator
- ☐ The First Lady
- ☐ The first kids
- ☐ The Prez's dog

Name

Grade

Best Friend

Fave Band

Fave Color

Fave Sport

Fave Movie

Fave Game

MY D.C.

My trip to D.C. will be:
- ☐Fantastic
- ☐Fine
- ☐So-so
- ☐Bo...ring

All About ME In D.C.

COLLECTOR

When I travel I like to collect:

- ◊ Postcards
- ◊ T-shirts
- ◊ Maps
- ◊ Pins
- ◊ Other

____

____

____

____

____

____

____

____

D.C. AND ME

Fun Fact - On the continental U.S., D.C. is the only place where U.S. citizens do not have a vote in Congress. ☐ Did you spot the D.C. license plate that says "Taxation without representation"? Should Washingtonians have the right to vote? ☐ Yes ☐ No

Getting Around D.C.

Bike It

◇ **Free Ranger Bike Tours**

In the summer, join National Park Service rangers each Saturday and Sunday.
www.nps.gov/mall/

◇ **Bike and Roll**

Rent a bike or take a guided bike tour. Start at Union Station, the Old Post Office or Alexandria.
www.bikethesites.com

◇ **Capital Bikeshare**

Are you 16 or older? For quick short trips, pick up a bike and drop it off at many locations around the city. Find out more:
www.capitalbikeshare.com

Tour It

◇ **Tourmobile**

All-day reboarding. Buy tickets from the driver at the National Mall and Arlington Cemetery stops.
www.tourmobile.com

◇ **D.C. Ducks**

Land and water tour on the boat with wheels. Buy tickets online or at Union Station.
www.DCducks.com

◇ **Old Town Trolley Tours**

Buy tickets online or at Union Station.
www.trolleytours.com

◇ **Open Top Sightseeing**

Buy tickets online or at Union Station.
www.opentopsightseeing.com

Prepare & Be Amazed

What's Up in D.C.?

◇ **Smithsonian Calendar**

Did you check out the Smithsonian's calendar? ◇Yes ◇No
You'll be amazed by what they have going on!
www.si.edu/events/

◇ **National Park Service**

Did you check out D.C. on NPS's website? ◇Yes ◇No
You'll be surprised by all the sights you can see.
www.nps.gov/state/DC/

GETTING THERE AND AWAY

Planes

The Washington, D.C. area has three major airports: Dulles, Reagan National, and BWI.

Have you flown in or out of D.C.? ◇Yes ◇No
Where did you land or take off?
◇ Dulles International, Virginia
◇ Ronald Reagan National, Virginia
◇ BWI, Thurgood Marshall, Maryland

Trains

Take Amtrak right into D.C.'s Union Station; it is just down the street from the U.S. Capitol and the National Mall.

Have you taken the train to or from D.C.? ◇Yes ◇No
Which train did you take?
◇ Amtrak
◇ Virginia Railway Express (VRE)
◇ Maryland Rail Commuter (MARC)

Automobiles

Have you driven into D.C.? ◇Yes ◇No
Which major highway did you take?
◇ **South** - Interstate 95 from Virginia
◇ **West** - Interstate 66 from Virginia
◇ **North** - Interstate 270 from Maryland
◇ **East** - Route 50 from Maryland
◇ **I live here, inside the Beltway**

... and Buses

Have you taken the bus into D.C.? ◇Yes ◇No
Which bus did you take?
◇Charter Bus ◇School Bus
◇Greyhound Bus ◇Other

MY TRAVEL PLANS

Fun fact - for almost 100 years streetcars traveled along the roads of D.C. In the 1800s, horse-drawn streetcars trotted along the flat roads. Then electric streetcars took over, climbing hills and going faster. The last streetcar ran in 1962. Do you wish there were still streetcars? ■ Yes ■ No

My Street smarts

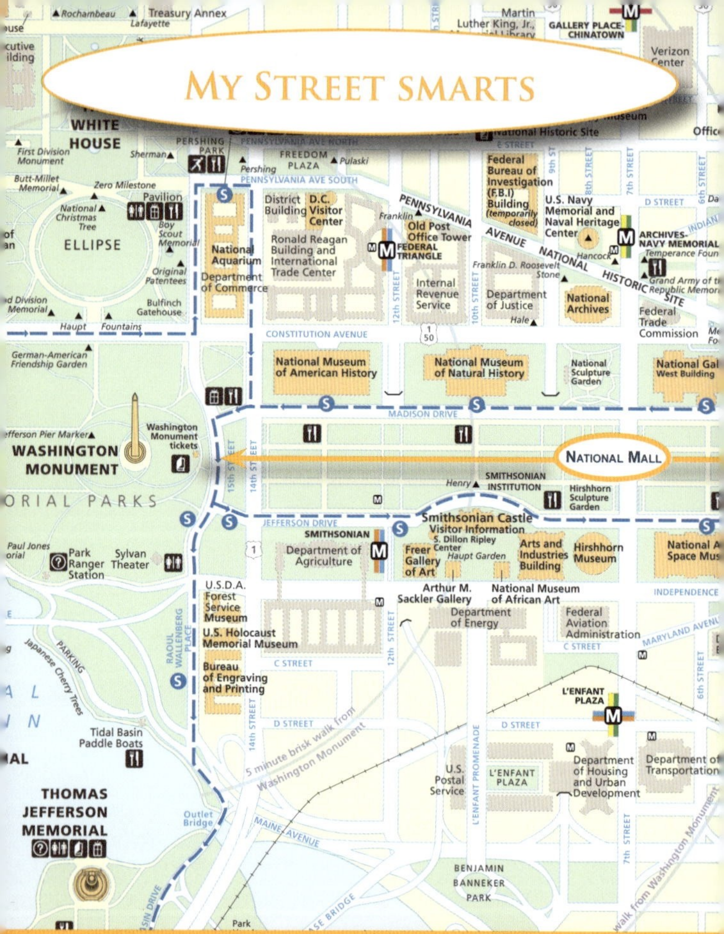

D.C. is split into 4 quadrants. The U.S. Capitol is the center point.

Street names repeat in each quadrant; therefore, all addresses in D.C. end with NW, NE, SW or SE.

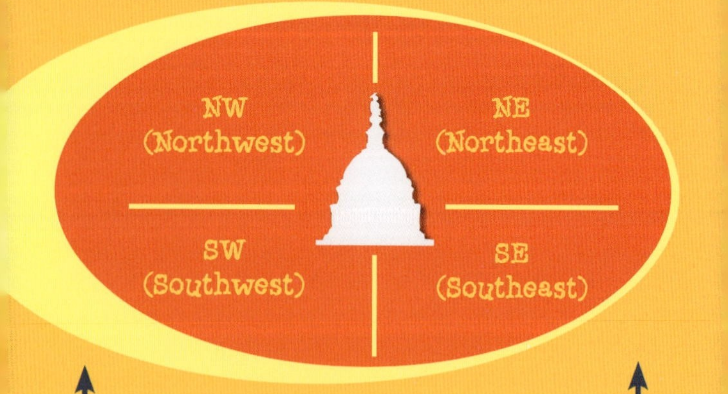

Numbers

All streets running north to south are numbered. There is a 1st street east of the Capitol. A completely different 1st St runs west of the Capitol. On the map, can you find 1st Street in each Quadrant?

○NW ○SW ○NE ○SE

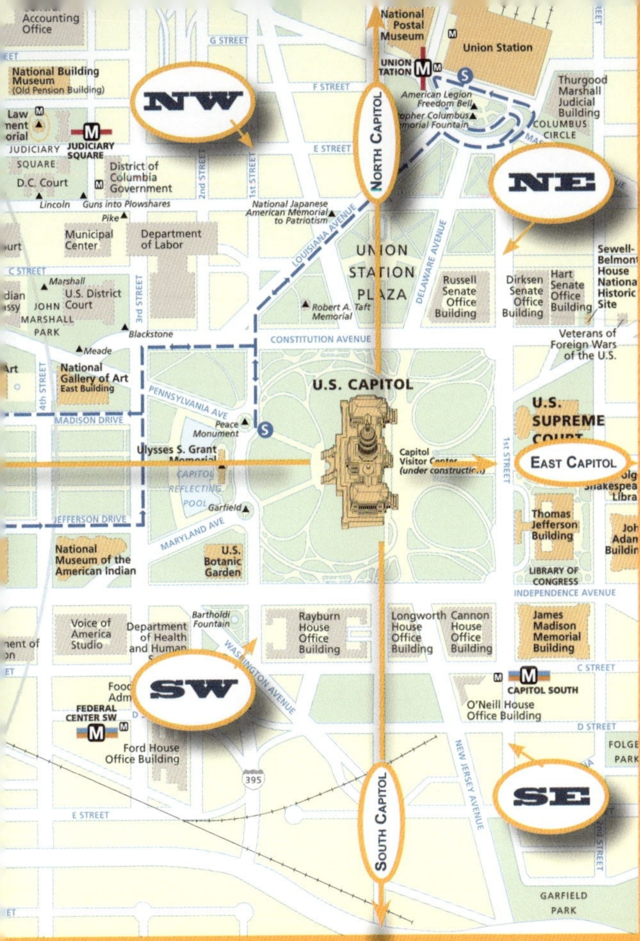

ALPHABET

ALL STREETS RUNNING EAST TO WEST ARE ALPHABETICAL. WHEN THE LETTERED STREETS OF A-W ARE FINISHED THE STREETS CONTINUE ALPHABETICALLY WITH ONE-SYLLABLE THEN TWO & THREE SYLLABLE NAMES. THERE ARE NO J, X, Y, OR Z STREETS IN ANY OF THE QUADRANTS.

STATES

MANY OF THE STREETS THAT RUN OUT OF TOWN LIKE THE SPOKES OF A WHEEL ARE STATE NAMES.

MY STREET SMARTS

D.C. was designed by Pierre L'Enfant. He created a grid system with 4 quadrants that meet at the center of the U.S. Capitol. The quadrants (Northwest, Southwest, Northeast, Southeast) are separated by North Capitol, South Capitol, and East Capitol Streets, and also the National Mall.

My Mall Map West

29
FARRAGUT
Farragut
SQUARE
McPHERSON
McPherson
SQUARE
McPHERSON SQUARE
FRANKLI
Barry
SQUARE
FARRAGUT WEST
St. John's Church
Department of Veterans Affairs
EDWARD R. MURROW PARK
H STREET
Von Steuben
Kosciuszko
Decatur House
New Executive Office Building
Renwick Gallery
Blair-Lee House
LAFAYETTE PARK
Baruch Bench
Jackson
Rochambeau
Lafayette
U.S. Court of Appeals and U.S. Court of Claims
Treasury Annex
NEW YORK AVENUE
19th STREET
18th STREET
Eisenhower Executive Office Building
East Executive Park
Department of the Treasury
G STREET
17th STREET
THE WHITE HOUSE
15th STREET
White House Visitor Center
General Services Administration
The Octagon
NEW YORK AVE
Corcoran Gallery of Art
First Division Monument
Rawlins
PERSHING PARK
Sherman
Pershing
PENNSYLVANIA AV
FREEDOM PLAZA
Butt-Millet Memorial
Zero Milestone
Department of the Interior Museum
American National Red Cross
D STREET
C STREET
Constitution Hall
Daughters of the American Revolution
Bolivar
National Christmas Tree
ELLIPSE
Pavilion
Boy Scout Memorial
National Aquarium
Department of Commerce
District Building
Ronald Re Building a Internatio Trade Cen
Original Patentees
Organization of American States
Organization of American States Annex
Artigas
Second Division Memorial
Haupt
Fountains
Bulfinch Gatehouse
CONSTITUTIO
Lock Keeper's House
German-American Friendship Garden
17th ST
The 56 Signers of the Declaration of Independence Memorial
NSTITUTION GARDENS
National of Ameri
Jefferson Pier Marker
Washington Monument tickets
WASHINGTON MONUMENT
World War II Memorial
15th STREET
14th STREET
L MALL & MEMORIAL PARKS
JEFFERSON D
Home Front Drive
John Paul Jones Memorial
Park Ranger Station
Sylvan Theater
Depart Agric
U.S.D.A. Forest Service Museum
U.S. Holocaust Memorial Museum
KUTZ BRIDGE
Japanese Lantern and First Cherry Tree Planting
Martin Luther King, Jr., Plaque (future memorial site)
PARKING
Japanese Cherry Trees
RAOUL WALLENBERG PLACE
C STREET
Bureau of Engraving and Printing
TIDAL BASIN
D STREET
Tidal Basin Paddle Boats
FRANKLIN DELANO ROOSEVELT MEMORIAL
5 minute brisk w Washington
THOMAS JEFFERSON MEMORIAL
Japanese Pagoda
Japanese Cherry Trees
Outlet Bridge
MAINE AVENUE
Inlet Bridge
EAST BASIN DRIVE
one-way
Park Headquarters
George Mason Memorial

MY MALL MAP EAST

K STREET
I STREET
H STREET
G STREET
F STREET
E STREET
D STREET
NORTH CAPITOL STREET
Government Printing Office
National Postal Museum
Union Station
UNION STATION
American Legion Freedom Bell
Christopher Columbus Memorial Fountain
Thurgood Marshall Judicial Building
COLUMBUS CIRCLE
MASSACHUSETTS AVE
2nd STREET
1st STREET
3rd STREET
District of Columbia Government
National Japanese American Memorial to Patriotism
LOUISIANA AVENUE
Department of Labor
UNION STATION PLAZA
DELAWARE AVENUE
Russell Senate Office Building
Dirksen Senate Office Building
Hart Senate Office Building
Robert A. Taft Memorial
Blackstone
CONSTITUTION AVENUE
Veterans of Foreign Wars of the U.S.
U.S. CAPITOL
PENNSYLVANIA AVE
Peace Monument
Ulysses S. Grant Memorial
CAPITOL REFLECTING POOL
Capitol Visitor Center (under construction)
U.S. SUPREME COURT
EAST CAPITOL STREET
Garfield
MARYLAND AVE
Thomas Jefferson Building
LIBRARY OF CONGRESS
U.S. Botanic Garden
INDEPENDENCE AVENUE
Bartholdi Fountain
Department of Health and Human Services
Rayburn House Office Building
Longworth House Office Building
Cannon House Office Building
James Madison Memorial Building
C STREET
WASHINGTON AVENUE
CAPITOL SOUTH
O'Neill House Office Building
Food and Drug Administration
Ford House Office Building
395
SOUTH CAPITOL STREET
NEW JERSEY AVENUE
NORTH CAROLINA AVENUE
E STREET
GARFIELD PARK
To Frederick Douglass National Historic Site and Anacostia Museum via Anacostia Bridge
MY D.C.

My Metro Map

Legend

- Red Line • Glenmont to Shady Grove
- Orange Line • New Carrollton to Vienna/Fairfax-GMU
- Blue Line • Franconia-Springfield to Largo Town Center
- Green Line • Branch Avenue to Greenbelt
- Yellow Line • Huntington to Fort Totten

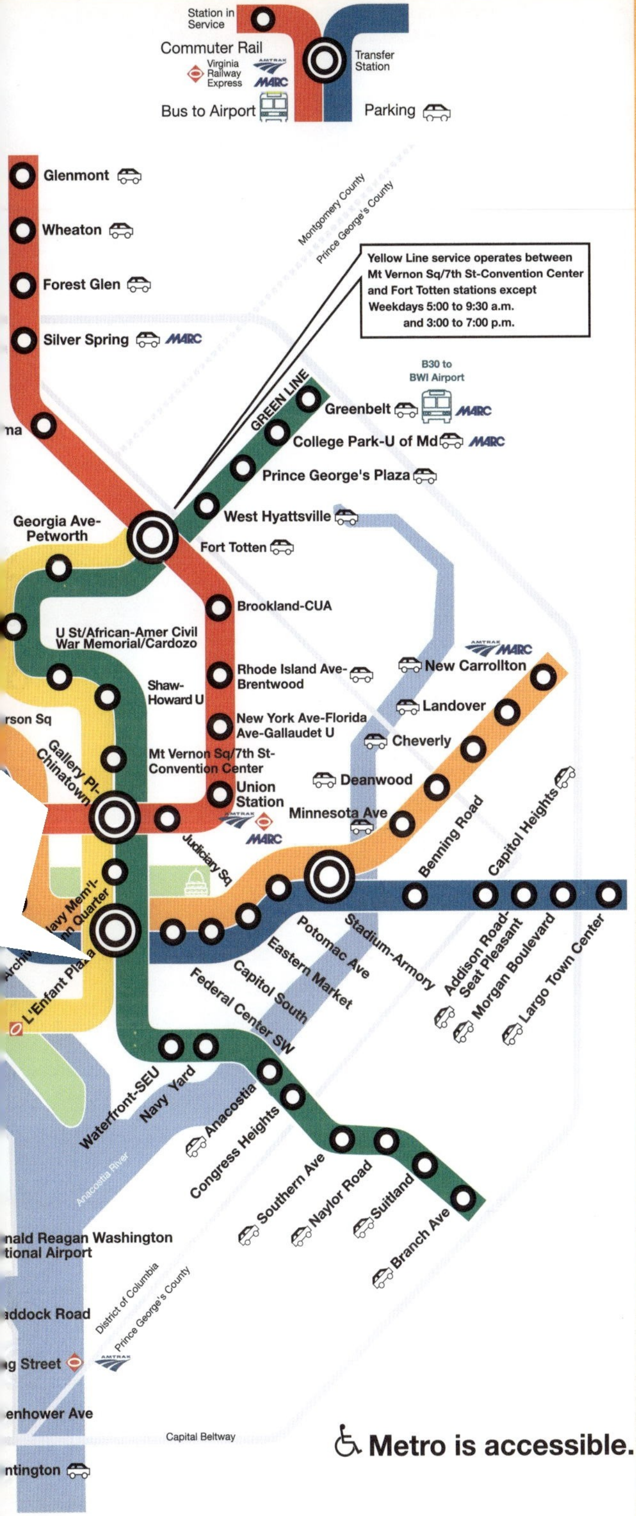

Hours of operation- Mon - Thurs 5 a.m. - 12 a.m.
Fri - Sat 7 a.m. - 3 a.m. Sun 7 a.m. - 12 a.m.

My D.C. Challenge

What can you see in D.C.? Check it off as you visit.

Capitol South
Blue and Orange Line

☐ US Capitol Visitors Center ☐ US Botanic Gardens
☐ Supreme Court ☐ Library of Congress
☐ Folger Shakespeare Library
☐ Eastern Market (walk a few blocks)

Archive/Navy Memorial Stop
Blue and Orange Line

☐ National Archives ☐ National Gallery of Art
☐ National Gallery Sculpture Garden and Ice Rink
☐ Newseum ☐ F.B.I. (closed to visitors)

Federal Triangle Stop Blue and Orange Line

☐ White House Visitors Center ☐ National Aquarium
☐ D.C. Visitors Center ☐ Old Post Office Pavilion

Farragut West Stop Blue and Orange Line

☐ Renwick Gallery ☐ Decatur House ☐ White House
☐ Lafayette Park ☐ Eisenhower Office Bldg
☐Corcoran ☐Red Cross ☐DAR Constitution Hall
☐Georgetown (bus transfer)

Grouped by Metro Stop

Union Station Stop Red Line

☐ Union Station ☐ National Postal Museum

Gallery Place/Chinatown Stop Red Line

☐ American Art Museum ☐ Portrait Gallery
☐ National Building Museum ☐ Spy Museum
☐ Chinatown ☐ Science Museum
☐ Museum of Crime and Punishment

Metro Center Stop Red Line

☐ Ford's Theatre ☐ Peterson House
☐ Museum of Women in the Arts

Dupont Circle Stop Red Line

☐ Dupont Circle ☐ Adams Morgan
☐ Textile Museum ☐ Fondo Del Sol Arts Center
☐ Woodrow Wilson House ☐ Phillips Collection
☐ Embassy Row ☐ National Geographic

Woodley Park/Zoo Stop Red Line

☐ National Zoological Park
☐ National Cathedral (bus transfer, cab it or walk)

Smithsonian Stop (North) - National Mall East
Blue and Orange Line
☐ Museum of the American Indian
☐ Air and Space ☐ Hirshhorn Museum
☐ Sculpture Garden ☐ Carousel ☐ The Castle
☐ Museum of African Art ☐ Freer Gallery
☐ Sackler Gallery of Art ☐ Enid A. Haupt Garden
☐ Ripley Center - Discovery Theatre
☐ Voice of America ☐ Museum of American History
☐ Museum of Natural History

Smithsonian Stop (South) - Tidal Basin
Blue and Orange Line
☐ Washington Monument ☐ Holocaust Museum
☐ Bureau of Printing and Engraving
☐ Tidal Basin ☐ Paddle Boats
☐ Japanese Cherry Trees ☐ Jefferson Memorial
☐ FDR Memorial ☐ MLK Memorial

Smithsonian Stop (North) - National Mall West
Or Foggy Bottom GWU Blue and Orange Line
☐ Lincoln Memorial ☐ Vietnam Veterans Memorial
☐ WWII Memorial ☐ Korean War Veterans Memorial

Virginia

Rosslyn Stop Blue and Orange Line
☐ Iwo Jima Memorial ☐ Teddy Roosevelt Island

Arlington Cemetery Stop Blue Line
☐ Arlington National Cemetery
☐ Robert E. Lee Memorial

Pentagon Stop Blue and Yellow Line
☐ The Pentagon Memorial

King Street Stop Blue and Yellow Line
☐ Old Town Alexandria ☐ GW Masonic Memorial

Huntington Stop Yellow Line
☐ Mount Vernon (bus transfer)

Get more information and upload photos at www.AllAboutMEinDC.com

My D.C. Challenge

Take the D.C. Challenge. There are so many sights to see in D.C., too many to fit in this book. We grouped them by Metro stop. As you visit, check them off. Visit our website to learn the rules and find out about prizes: www.AllAboutMEinDC.com

Did you know, D.C.'s record high temperature was 106°F? (July 1930)

Did you know, D.C.'s record low temperature was -15°F? (February 1899)

AVERAGE TEMPERATURES IN D.C.

Jan	Feb	Mar	Apr	May	Jun
42	47	56	66	75	84
27	30	37	46	56	65

Jul	Aug	Sep	Oct	Nov	Dec
88	86	79	68	57	47
70	69	62	50	40	32

TRAVEL SMART

What month are you visiting D.C.? ________

Average High °F __________ Low °F ________

How many days are you staying? _________

WHAT WOULD YOU PACK FOR DAY TIME?

SHOES
☐Boots
☐Sneakers
☐Sandals

GEAR
☐Jacket ☐Hat
☐Sunglasses

WHAT WOULD YOU PACK FOR NIGHT TIME?

SHOES
☐Boots
☐Sneakers
☐Sandals

GEAR
☐Jacket ☐Hat
☐Sunglasses

www.AllAboutMEinDC.com

Summer time weather forecast:
hazy, hot, and humid.
Chance of afternoon thunderstorms.

July is the hottest month

January is the coldest month

May can be the rainiest month

Winter time weather forecast:
mild, about 40-50 degrees.
Dress in layers and bring a winter coat.

D.C. IS ALL ABOUT WALKING

What is your most comfy pair of shoes?
My fave shoes are:

- ☐ Flip Flops
- ☐ Hiking Boots
- ☐ Sneakers
- ☐ Sandals
- ☐ Other

PACKING

Did you pack:

- ☐ Too much?
- ☐ Too little?
- ☐ Just right.
- ☐ I live here.

MY WEATHER

The spring in Washington, D.C. can be very cold one day and really hot the next day. If you are coming in March, April or May you will need to dress in layers and bring a rain coat. It's a great time to visit, but the weather can change quickly.

My Itinerary

You're the boss, build your own itinerary. An itinerary is a travel plan. Where would you go first? We suggest building your itinerary by area. That way you see the most without having to travel too far.

Preview the city first. Which would you choose?

◊ **Your maps** - Go to the D.C. Challenge. We have listed the main sights by Metro stop. Pick an area, then use the maps at the beginning of the book to chart your course.

◊ **The Tourmobile** -It's not free, but it is an easy way to see the sights and hear the history of D.C. Then you can decide what you just can't miss. www.tourmobile.com

◊ **By Car**- Do a driving tour of D.C. first. This takes preparation. With your map, chart a course. Ask your parents to go by each major monument and museum. Be the family tour guide; as you drive by each sight give a fun fact.

D.C. Fun Fact

Forty milestones mark D.C.'s original border.

Can you spot a boundary stone?

My Itinerary

1. :Start time
:End time

2. :Start time
:End time

3. :Start time
:End time

4. :Start time
:End time

5. :Start time
:End time

6. :Start time
:End time

7. :Start time
:End time

8. :Start time
:End time

9. :Start time
:End time

10. :Start time
:End time

My Itinerary

Give yourself time, don't rush it:

- 1-2 hours for each major museum.
- 2-3 hours for the National Zoo.
- Give time to visit exhibits and gift shops.
- Add travel time. Even walking takes time.

Pack your fave snacks and a water bottle.

The Smithsonian is the world's largest museum complex with 19 museums, 9 research centers, and the National Zoo. Admission to all Smithsonian museums is free.

Plan Your Visit to the Smithsonian

Start at the Castle. Did you see the:
☐ Orientation Video ☐ Hands-on Exhibits
Plan your visit online at www.gosmithsonian.com
For $2, buy *Go Smithsonian* at any museum.

Check off the sights as you visit them

Check off the museums as you visit them. Rate each. Give them one star, five stars, or somewhere in between.

- ☐ Museum of the American Indian ☆☆☆☆☆
- ☐ Air and Space Museum ☆☆☆☆☆
- ☐ Hirshhorn Museum & Garden ☆☆☆☆☆
- ☐ Arts and Industries (Closed) ☆☆☆☆☆
- ☐ Carousel on the Mall ☆☆☆☆☆
- ☐ The Castle ☆☆☆☆☆
- ☐ Enid A. Haupt Garden ☆☆☆☆☆
- ☐ Museum of African Art ☆☆☆☆☆
- ☐ Sackler Gallery of Art ☆☆☆☆☆
- ☐ Ripley Center ☆☆☆☆☆
- ☐ Discovery Theater ☆☆☆☆☆
- ☐ Freer Gallery of Art ☆☆☆☆☆
- ☐ Museum of American History ☆☆☆☆☆
- ☐ Museum of Natural History ☆☆☆☆☆
- ☐ Postal Museum ☆☆☆☆☆
- ☐ American Art Museum ☆☆☆☆☆
- ☐ Portrait Gallery ☆☆☆☆☆
- ☐ Renwick Gallery ☆☆☆☆☆
- ☐ National Zoo ☆☆☆☆☆
- ☐ Anacostia Community Museum ☆☆☆☆☆

R.I.P.

In 1829, at age 64, James Smithson died. Smithson mysteriously left his fortune to America, even though he had never visited here. His fortune sailed by ship to Philadelphia in 11 treasure boxes filled with 104,960 gold coins. All but two coins were melted down to be worth $508,318. Smithson wanted his fortune to found "... an establishment for the increase and diffusion of knowledge..." Mission accomplished! He rests in peace at the Castle.

SMITHSONIAN

My Fave Five at the Smithsonian

1.

2.

3.

4.

5.

My Smithsonian

At the Smithsonian which did you like best?

- National Zoo
- Air and Space
- Natural History

What is your favorite object at the Smithsonian?

If you could take any object home from the Smithsonian what would it be?

What job would you do at the Smithsonian?

- Curator
- Historian
- Scientist

Castle & More

Smithsonian Institute Castle
1000 Jefferson Drive SW, Washington, D.C.
Admission Free. Website www.si.edu
Hours 8:30 a.m. - 5: 30 p.m. Closed Christmas.
Metro - Smithsonian (Mall exit)

If YOU could...

be in charge, what kind of museum would YOU create?

You can spend as much money as you want. Pick an overall theme. Then pick sub themes. Each room/exhibit can be a sub theme.

Theme -

Sub theme #1-

Sub theme #2 -

Sub theme #3-

You make the rules.

Design your own museum. Fill it with stuff that you like.

How will you make money to run the museum?

◇Admission ◇Restaurants
◇Gift Shops ◇IMAX theatre
◇ Ice Cream Parlor ◇ Simulators
◇ Other______________________

How would you show off your collection? ◇ Virtual Reality Experience ◇ Famous Objects ◇ Interactive Games ◇ Hands on Exhibits ◇ Live Shows ◇ Other______________________

Draw your own floor plan. Will your museum be:

□ Round □ Square □ Octagonal

SMITHSONIAN

Natural History Dinosaurs

Fossil Lab - Did you see the paleontologists at work? If you were a paleontologist, what fossils would you study?

O Dinosaurs O Ancient Seas
O Mammal Fossils O Plant Fossils

Dino Digger Character Traits

Check off traits that describe you.

O patient O passion for fossils
O detail focused O curious mind
O team player O problem solver

Would you be a paleontologist?

O Yes O No

Discover The Ocean Hall

I'm Phoenix,
the Ocean Hall Ambassador.
Why did they name me after the mythical bird that burned but rose from the ashes? I almost died, but I lived to swim another day. What happened to me?

☐ Tangled in fishing gear ☐ Hunters ☐ Ship Collision

We are endangered. About how many North Atlantic Right Whales are left in the wild?

☐ 10,000 ☐ 6,200 ☐ 400

Mammal Hall

Mammals have hair, can control their body temperature, and can feed their babies milk, but mostly do NOT lay eggs. Humans are mammals.

● True ● False

My Fave Five at Natural History

1.
2.
3.
4.
5.

HOPE DIAMOND

Is the Hope Diamond curse really true? Has it *brought trouble to all who have owned it?* O Yes O No

HUMAN ORIGINS

Why do we get goosebumps? If we still had body hair it would stand up when we get:
O cold O scared O all of the above
Now, since we don't have much body hair, all we are left with are goosebumps! Check out Human Origins to learn more.

THE GIANT SQUID

They are deep sea dwellers, rarely ever seen and can grow to over 6 times the size of grown-up humans.

Did you see the boy and girl Giant Squid?
⚪Yes ⚪No
Which was bigger?
⚪ BOY
⚪ GIRL

th MAX Theater? ⚪Yes

Film name:

Butterfly Pavilion? ⚪Yes

Answers: Tangled in a net, 400, True - you can kill coral if you step on them, True - coral are animals, True - we are mammals, No - the curse is a myth.

NATURAL HISTORY

National Museum of Natural History
10th Street and Constitution Ave., NW
Hours 8:30 a.m. - 5: 30 p.m. Closed Christmas.
Admission Free. www.mnh.si.edu
Metro - Smithsonian (Mall exit)

Whas up?

Did you visit the Discovery Room at the Museum of Natural History? ☐ Yes ☐ No

Did you touch cool stuff? ☐ Yes ☐ No

Did you visit the Orkin Insect Zoo? ☐ Yes ☐ No

Your Space

Write your memories, doodle or use it as a pillow! This is your space. You make the rules!

SMITHSONIAN

WHAT'S THE STORY?

Hunt for the objects at American History. Check them off.
Find out the real story behind each object.

☐ **STAR SPANGLED BANNER**
Why is this flag so important:
☐ Size ☐ Inspired the national anthem

☐ **LINCOLN'S HAT**
Abe used his hat to: ☐ shade himself ☐ carry his papers

☐ **JULIA CHILD'S KITCHEN**
Julia Child used this kitchen:
☐ to cook for her family
☐ as a TV studio

☐ **1903 WINTON**
This car is important because:
☐ it was the first car driven across the United States
☐ Bud the dog rode in the car and wore goggles

☐ **KERMIT THE FROG**
What are Kermit's eyes made of?
☐ foam balls ☐ ping pong balls

☐ **DOROTHY'S RUBY SLIPPERS**
When Dorothy tapped her slippers together she said:
☐ There's no place like home
☐ Toto, we're not in Kansas anymore

☐ **MUHAMMAD ALI'S BOXING GLOVES**
Muhammad Ali was first named:
☐ Cassius Clay ☐ "The Greatest"

☐ **GREENSBORO LUNCH COUNTER**
Why is this lunch counter at American History:
☐ famous civil rights sit-in ☐ a place to have lunch

☐ **EDISON "NEW YEAR'S EVE" LAMP**
Why is this carbon-filament bulb highlighted:
☐ Edison's first public showing of his invention
☐ Edison was the only inventor of the light bulb

Answers: Inspired the national anthem, carry his papers, as a TV studio, it was the first car driven across the United States, ping pong balls, There's no place like home, Cassius Clay, famous civil rights sit-in, Edison's first public showing of his invention.

My American History

Which exhibit did you like best?

- National Treasures
- Hall of Invention
- Artifact Walls

What is your favorite object at American History?

Do you like to research and tell stories? Yes / No

How would you tell your American history stories?

- Write
- Sing
- Make a video

How will you make history? What will you be?

- Inventor
- Athlete
- Scientist

My Fave Five at Spark!Lab & Inventions at Play

(two interactive exhibits that explore inventing)

1.
2.
3.
4.
5.

Inventor's Doodles

Doodling is another way to think and find solutions. What were you inspired to invent? Doodle it here.

American History

National Museum of American History
14th Street and Constitution Ave. NW
Hours 8:30 a.m. - 5: 30 p.m. Closed Christmas.
Admission Free. www.americanhistory.si.edu
Metro - Smithsonian or Federal Triangle

Fave Five Inventions

What are the top five inventions that YOU couldn't live without? List them, then write one way that YOU would make them better. Be imaginative.

1. ______________________________

I would make it better by ______________________

____

____

____

2. ______________________________

I would make it better by ______________________

____

____

____

3. ______________________________

I would make it better by ______________________

____

____

____

4. ______________________________

I would make it better by ______________________

____

____

____

5. ______________________________

I would make it better by ______________________

____

____

____

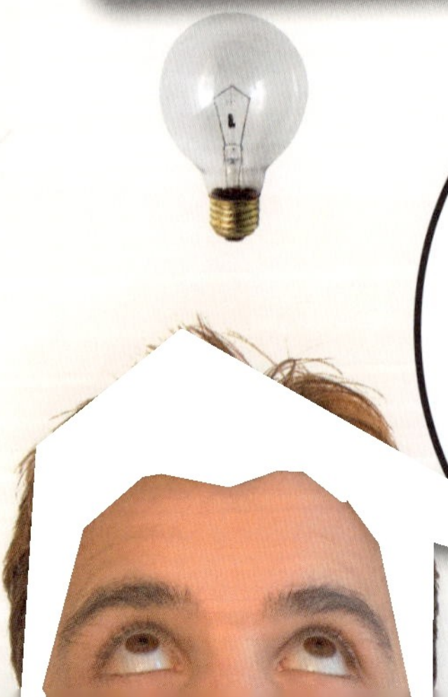

Your Space

Write your ideas, doodle or make a shopping list! This is your space. You make the rules!

N

My Air and Space

If you could go into space how would you get there?

- Rocket
- Space Shuttle
- SpaceShipOne

What film did you see at the IMAX Theater?

Did you see the 1903 Wright Flyer? Yes No

If you were a pilot who would you work for?

- The Airlines
- The Navy
- The Post Office

What job in aeronautics would you like to do?

- Pilot
- Rocket Scientist
- Astronaut

Public Observatory

Outside on the building's east terrace, look through a daytime telescope and see the moon, the planets, and the sun (safely). For hours check at NASM welcome desk or www.nasm.si.edu

Do you have...

Space Race

What 2 countries were in a race to get to the moon?

☐USSR & USA

☐China & USA

The space race was between USSR (Russia) & USA. USSR was first into space. USA was first to put a man on the moon. USA won the space race.

Milestones of Flight

What came first in the history of flight? Number them from 1-8. Can you spot these aircraft at Air and Space?

___Bell X-1	___ Jet Plane
___Wright Flyer	___ Hot Air Balloon
___Space Shuttle	___ Lunar Lander
___Spirit of St. Louis	___ Kite

1.

2.

3.

4.

5.

...the right stuff?

Memorize the Planets:
My Very Enthusiastic Mother Just Served Us Noodles

In the above sentence, the first letter in each word represents a planet, starting with the planet closest to the sun.

Did this help you memorize the planets? ☐ Yes ☐ No

Did you visit the Einstein Planetarium? ☐ Yes ☐ No

Air and Space

National Air and Space Museum National Mall
National Air and Space Museum Hazy Center
Admission Free - Closed Christmas Day
Hours 8:30 a.m. - 5: 30 p.m. Summer - till 7:30
Metro - Smithsonian or L'Enfant Plaza
www.nasm.si.edu

If You Could...

discover alien life forms in another galaxy, what would you want to tell them about Earth?

Your Space

This is your space.
You make the rules!
Draw, dream
and discover all
that your imagination
has to offer.

MY BLUE PLANET VS. MARS THE RED PLANET

Oxygen: Earth - Yes   Mars - No
Water: Earth is 70% water - On Mars frozen water has been discovered.
Do you think humans could terraform Mars (to make another planet earth-like or livable) and inhabit it? O Yes O No
If you were asked to go on a mission to Mars, would you go? O Yes   O No
What 3 things would you bring?

1.______________________________

2. _________________________

3.____________________

A Martian year is 687 days. An Earth year is 365 days. (A year is the time it takes a planet to orbit the sun.) If you were a Martian, about how old would you be in Mars years? _______

In Milestones of Flight did you see the Viking Lander, the first spacecraft to operate on Mars? O Yes   O No

Scavenger Hunt

If you find similar objects at the museum, circle them. Write the number on the line that best describes the object:

___ Beaded Moccasins ___ Tomahawk ___ Canoe
___ Totem Pole ___ Arrowhead
___ Dreamcatcher ___ Native American Flute

answers: 7,5,4,6,1,2,3

Did all Native Americans:

Canoe? O Yes O No
Use bows and arrows? O Yes O No
Have powwows? O Yes O No
Use tomahawks? O Yes O No
Carve totem poles? O Yes O No
Do rain dances? O Yes O No
Make dreamcatchers? O Yes O No

If you answered <u>No</u> to all these questions, you are correct! Native American tribes and people were and are all very different. Did you find the book *Do All Indians Live in Tipis?* in the Learning Center and gift shop? O Yes O No

SMITHSONIAN

Code Talkers

During World War I and II, Native Americans joined the U.S. armed forces to become code talkers. They created a code by choosing a Navajo word for each letter in the English alphabet.

Letter	Navajo Word	English Word
A	Wol-la-chee	Ant
C	Moasi	Cat
D	Lha-cha-eh	Dog
E	Dzeh	Elk
K	Klizzie-yazzie	Kid
L	Dibeh-yazzie	Lamb
O	Ne-ahs- jah	Owl
R	Gah	Rabbit
T	Than-zie	Turkey

Can You Break the Code?

Moasi Ne-ahs-jah Lha-cha-eh Dzeh
Than-zie Wol-la-chee Dibeh-yazzie
Klizzie-yazzie Dzeh Gah

_ _ _ _   _ _ _ _ _ _

To hear the whole story go to
www.americanindian.si.edu/education/codetalkers/

answer: code talker

My Fave Five at American Indian

1.

2.

3.

4.

5.

American Indian

National Museum of the American Indian
Fourth Street & Independence Ave., S.W.
Hours 10 a.m. - 5:30 p.m. Closed Christmas Day
Admission Free - www.nmai.si.edu
Metro - L'Enfant Plaza (Maryland Avenue Exit)

Totem Pole

Did you know...Native people of the Pacific Northwest carved monumental sculptures called totem poles. They used one large tree. Not many poles from before 1900 exist because they decayed or were bought or stolen.

Doodle your own Totem Pole

On the opposite page check off which character traits describe you best. Pick which animal spirits you want to add to your totem pole.

WHALE

O Wise
O Smart
O Kind

BEAVER

O Loyal
O Successful
O Instinctive

RAVEN

O Curious
O Mischievous
O Courageous

HAWK

O Helper
O Healer
O Visionary

OWL

O Insightful
O Sneaky
O Messenger

FROG

O Energetic
O Sensitive
O Water loving

EAGLE

O Leader
O Creator
O All-powerful

THUNDERBIRD

O Fire loving
O Mischievous
O Courageous

WOLF

O Loyal
O Successful
O Instinctive

BEAR

O Energetic
O Sensitive
O Water

S M I T H S O N I A N

Pandas At the Zoo

The giant panda is a rare bear and one of the world's most threatened animals. Pandas live in a small area in China and only eat bamboo. Protecting the bamboo forests can help save the pandas.

How many hours a day do pandas need to eat bamboo? ☐ 3 ☐ 6 ☐ 12

Elephant Trail

What species of elephant can you see at the Zoo?
☐ Asian ☐ African
How can you tell the difference between an African and Asian elephant? ☐ Ears ☐ Trunk
☐ All of the above

Amazonia - It's a Jungle

As you enter this tropical jungle, be careful, the rays might spit at you. Visit the amazing 55,000-gallon aquarium. Don't miss the piranhas. Trek through the jungle, spot a two-toed sloth.

Rainforests cover about 2% of the Earth. What percentage of the Earth's plants and animals live there? ☐ 2% ☐ 10% ☐ 50%

Reptiles

Reptiles can live longer than you. The Aldabra tortoise can live for 150 years. Think before you get one as a pet.
Which of these animals is not a reptile?
☐ Snake ☐ Toad ☐ Turtle
☐ Crocodile ☐ Chameleon

Primates

Primates include humans, apes, monkeys and lemurs. Visit your cousins the primates at Lemur Island, the Great Ape House, Gibbon Ridge and the Think Tank.
What's the difference between most apes and monkeys?
☐ Tail ☐ Brain size ☐ All of the above

& The Asia Trail

On the Asia Trail at the zoo, you'll see not one panda, but two; fishing cats that love to swim; red pandas that snooze on a limb; a family of otters that love to play; sloth bears that nap all day; a clouded leopard that can really climb, and a Japanese giant salamander all covered in slime.

Bird House

What bird can be 5 feet tall, but only weigh 5 pounds? F L _ M _ N G _.
How do these birds get their pink color? Are they born with it?

My Zoo

What animal would you work to save from extinction?
○ Panda ○ Tiger ○ Elephant ○ Gorilla ○ Orangutan

If you could travel & study animals where would you go?
○ Europe ○ Asia ○ Africa ○ U.S.A. ○ Australia

Do you think being a zookeeper is fun? ○ Yes ○ No

What job at the Zoo would you do?
○ Zoologist ○ Veterinarian ○ Zookeeper

My Fave Five Invertebrates

What were your FAVE FIVE at the Invertebrate House?

DID YOU KNOW, 95% OF ALL ANIMALS ARE INVERTEBRATES?

1.
2.
3.
4.
5.

Answers - left page: Pandas eat bamboo for 12 hours a day, Asian elephants, African elephants have bigger ears and two fingerlike features on the end of their trunk, 50% of the animals live in rainforests, Toads are amphibians, All of the above. Right page: Flamingo, flamingos are not born pink, their color is from the food they eat.

National Zoo

National Zoological Park
3001 Connecticut Ave. NW
Admission Free - Closed Christmas Day
Hours: call 202-633-4800 or visit
www.nationalzoo.si.edu
Metro - Cleveland Park or Woodley Park/Zoo

SMITHSONIAN

My Zoo Challenge

Did you know, there are over 2,000 animals at the Zoo.
One duty of a zookeeper is to observe the animals.
Are you talented at spotting animals? ☐ Yes ☐ No
Did you check the daily programs and feedings? ☐ Yes ☐ No

Directions:

√ First check off which habitats you visit.

√ Then check off what animals you see.

𝍸 Finally, using hatch marks note how many you see!

Visit the Birds

◯ **Bird House – It's gone to the birds**

What were your fave 5 birds? ______

______ ______

______ ______

● _____ Flamingos. Are there too many to count? Try or take a guess – write it on the line above. Ask a zookeeper

What is the world's only so-called wingless bird? It i New Zealand and is nocturnal. K _ W _ . It has its special room; can you find it at the Bird House? ☐

Along the Olmstead Walk

◯ **Small Mammals House – Our smallest cousins**

◯ ___Tamarin ◯ ___Ferret ◯ ___Porcupine ◯ ___ Fennec fox
◯ ___Armadillo ◯ ___Naked mole-rat ◯ ___Shrew

◯ **Great Apes, Gibbon Ridge & Think Tank – No tails**

◯ ___ Gibbons ◯ ___Gorillas ◯ ___Orangutans ◯ ___Macaques

◯ **Reptile Discovery Ctr – A cold blooded bunch**

◯ ___ Lizards ◯ ___Snakes ◯ ___Crocodilians ◯ ___ Sirens
◯ ___Frogs & Toads ◯ ___ Newts ◯ ___Turtles & Tortoises

◯ **Invertebrate House – They have no backbone**

◯ ___Corals ◯ ___Jellyfish ◯ ___Octopus ◯ ___Crustaceans
◯ ___Shellfish ◯ ___Ants ◯ ___Spiders ◯ ___Bees & Butterflies

At the Top

Asia Trail – Pandas, Otters and more

___Pandas ___Otters ___Red Pandas ___Salamander
___Clouded Leopards ___Fishing Cats ___Sloth Bears

Cheetah Conservation Station – Fast and Furry

___ Zebras ___Oryx ___Cheetahs ___Gazelles

Elephant House – Protecting Pachyderms

___ Kandula ___Shanti ___Ambika

At the Bottom

Great Cats and Leaping Lemur Island

___ Lions ___Tigers ___Lemurs

Kids Farm – Down on the Farm

___Alpacas ___Cows ___Goats ___Donkeys ___Pigs

Amazonia – Trek through the Amazon

___Monkeys ___ Piranhas ___ Stingrays ___Arapaimas
___Sloths ___Snakes ___Turtles ___Frogs ___Birds

Beaver Valley – Our North American Natives

___ Beavers ___Seals ___Sea Lions ___Otters
___Brown Pelicans ___Mexican Wolves ___Ducks

SMITHSONIAN

National Zoo

National Zoological Park
3001 Connecticut Ave. NW
Admission Free - Closed Christmas Day
Hours: call 202-633-4800 or visit
www.nationalzoo.si.edu
Metro - Cleveland Park or Woodley Park/Zoo

Got a question?

Write it down.

Why are poison dart frogs so colorful?

Where is George Washington buried?

Are you good at researching on the Web?

☐ Yes ☐ No

What websites do you like best?

Visit www.AllAboutMEinDC.com

Need an answer?

Did you ask a Ranger or expert?

□ Yes □ No

If yes, what did they say?

Do you like to go to the library?

□ Yes □ No

What books can you find on the subject?

Inside the Capitol

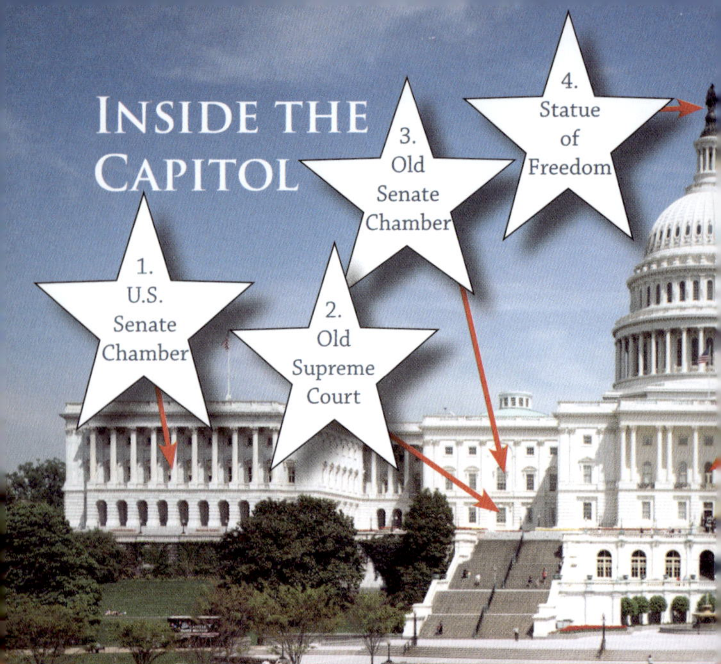

Myth or Fact?

1. Pierre L'Enfant picked the spot for the U.S. Capitol high on a hill.
   - Myth
   - Fact

2. George Washington is entombed below the Crypt of the Capitol.
   - Myth
   - Fact

3. The Capitol dome is made of marble.
   - Myth
   - Fact

4. The current and newest dome was built to be fire-proof.
   - Myth
   - Fact

5. The Statue of Freedom is a Native American woman.
   - Myth
   - Fact

6. No building in D.C. can be taller than the U.S. Capitol.
   - Myth
   - Fact

7. House members must be born in America.
   - Myth
   - Fact

8. Special flags that are flown over the Capitol can be requested.
   - Myth
   - Fact

9. Soldiers slept in the Capitol during the Civil War.
   - Myth
   - Fact

1. Fact. 2. Myth, a tomb was built for him, but he is buried at Mount Vernon. 3. Myth, it is made of cast iron. 4. Fact, but it turned out the metal could melt at high temperatures. 5. Myth, she has feathers on her helmet, but is a classical figure. 6. Myth, there is no law that states this, but few buildings are taller because of a height limitation law. 7. Myth, you must be a citizen for 7 years. 8. Fact. 9. Fact.

WE THE PEOPLE

Match 9 Capitol Hot Spots to the description that fits best. Write the # in the circle.

- The Senate NOW meets here. Senators serve a six year term. ◯
- A round room under the Rotunda with 40 columns that support the floor of the Rotunda. ◯
- It is 288 feet tall, and is made of 8,909,200 lbs of cast iron, painted to look like marble. ◯
- The round room under the Capitol dome. ◯
- Each state gives 2 statues to Congress.They are displayed here and around the Capitol. ◯
- This semicircular, half-domed chamber was first used by the Senate. ◯
- This was the Supreme Court's first chamber before it had its own building. ◯
- The House of Representatives NOW meets here. House members serve a two year term. ◯
- This statue sits atop the Capitol dome and weighs about 15,000 pounds. ◯

Answers top to bottom 1, 6, 5, 7, 8, 3, 2, 9, 4.

U.S. Capitol

First Street and East Capitol Street, NE
Hours 8:30 a.m. to 4:30 p.m. Mon-Sat
Closed Thanksgiving, Christmas, New Year's Day.
Reserve tickets for tours www.visitthecapitol.gov
Metro - Capitol South or Union Station

If You Could...

have the honor of being a be a painter in the U.S Capitol, where would you paint your masterpiece? What would you paint?

Master of Illusion

Over a 25 year period, Constantino Brumidi was the U.S. Capitol's master of illusion. He made paintings look 3-dimensional. At the U.S. Capitol, did you spot paintings by Brumidi?

- ☐ The Frieze of American History
- ☐ Apotheosis of Washington
- ☐ Brumidi Corridors

☐ The Frieze of American History

These 19 scenes circle the rotunda and tell America's story from Christopher Columbus to the Wright Brothers and the *Birth of Aviation.*

What is the defintion of a frieze?

O A kind of stone carving.

O A decorative band along the upper part of a wall.

What is the Frieze of American History made of?

O Paint O Stone

To see a panorama of the painting go to: www.aoc.gov and do a search for FRIEZE.

☐ Apotheosis of Washington

This painting is how many feet above the floor?

O 180 O 60 O 1000

Can you spot George Washington in this painting?

O Yes O No

What does Apotheosis mean?

O To elevate a person to the status of a god.

O To be a hero.

Would you paint on scaffolding 180 feet high?

O Yes O No

Answers: A decorative band along the upper part of a wall.• Painted to look like stone • 180 feet • To elevate a person to the status of a god.

Are You Afraid of Heights?

Did you know... At 73 years old Constantino Brumidi started painting the Frieze of American History above the U.S. Capitol Rotunda. While painting the scene "Settlement of Pennsylvania" Brumidi slipped off the scaffold and hung 58 feet above the ground until he was rescued. Sadly, he only came back to the scaffold once after the accident and died a few months later in February 1880. All in all, it took two more painters to finish this high flying work of art. It was not finished until 1953.

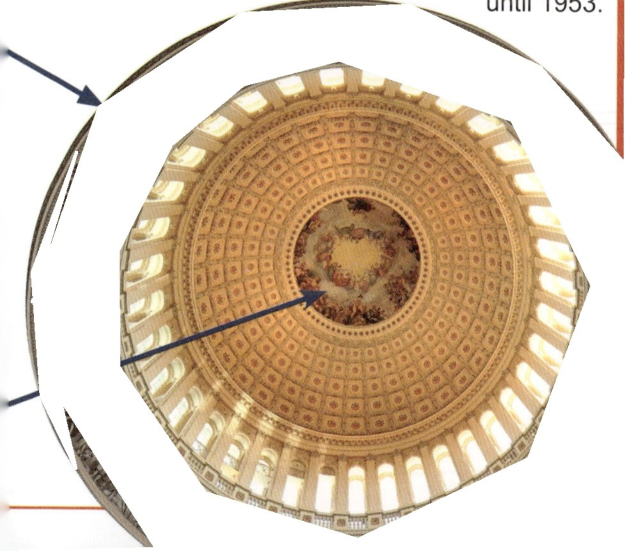

In the Guinness Book of World Records

The Library of Congress is the largest library in the world with the most shelf space (745 miles of bookshelves).

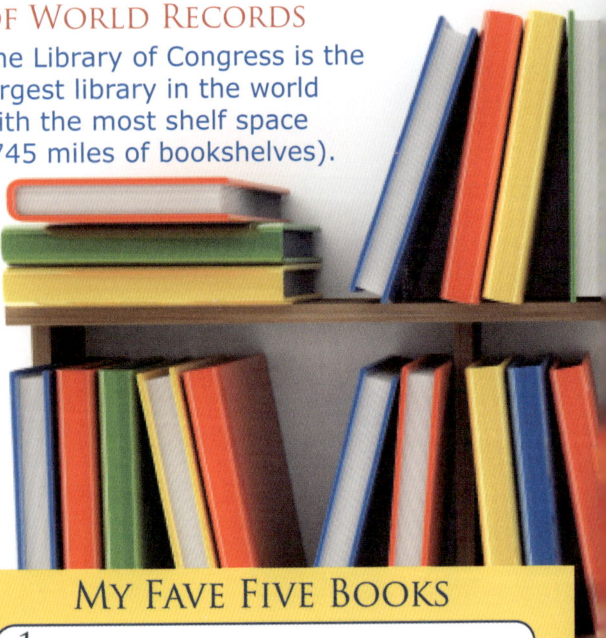

My Fave Five Books

1.
2.
3.
4.
5.

The first Library of Congress was in the U.S. Capitol. ☐ True ☐ False

In the War of 1812 the British set the U.S. Capitol on fire. The first Library of Congress was burned. How did I help start the new library?

★ I designed the building. ☐ True ☐ False

★ I sold my library to Congress. ☐ True ☐ False

The Jefferson building is one of the most beautiful buildings in America.

Can you spot the Putti figures: (little boys carved into the Great Hall's staircase). Each is holding a symbol of a job. Spot these three professions:

☐ Electrician ☐ Doctor ☐ Astronomer

Find out more: www.AllAboutMEinDC.com

Can YOU check out a book at the Library of Congress?

○ Yes ○ No

MY BOOKS AND WRITING

What is your favorite kind of book?

○ Sci-Fi ○ Fantasy ○ Myth ○ Mystery/Suspense

If you were a travel writer, where would you go?

○ Europe ○ Asia ○ Africa ○ U.S.A. ○ Australia

Do you think being a writer is fun? ○ Yes ○ No

What are you passionate about?

____

What kinds of books would you like to write?

○ Novels ○ Children's Books ○ Non-Fiction

Do you have a library in your room? What does it tell you about yourself? I am...

Write a character trait

Did you sit down and read at the Young Readers Center? ○ Yes ○ No

Did you visit "Knowledge Quest" before your visit? ○ Yes ○ No

www.myloc.gov/Pages/KnowledgeQuest.aspx

Answers - left page: True, False, True. Right page: No, the general public can not check out a book, it's a research library. Anyone 16 or older may use the collections.

LIBRARY OF CONGRESS

101 Independence Ave, SE
Hours 8:30 a.m. - 4: 30 p.m. Closed Sundays, Thanksgiving Day, Christmas & New Year's Day
Admission Free - www.myloc.gov
Metro - Capitol South

WE THE PEOPLE

If You Could...

be a famous best-selling author what would you write about?

Your Space

Use this as a diary page, doodle or write an award winning play! This is your space. You make the rules!

Me, Myself and I
I would rather...

WRITE ☐ a poem **OR** ☐ an essay
READ ☐ fiction **OR** ☐ non-fiction
CREATE A ☐ comic book **OR** ☐ graphic novel
NARRATE ☐ a story **OR** ☐ a play
DO ☐ crossword puzzles **OR** ☐ wordfinds
BROWSE ☐ a magazine **OR** ☐ a newspaper
READ ABOUT ☐ history **OR** ☐ mythology
SURF ☐ Yahoo **OR** ☐ Google
EDIT ☐ my work **OR** ☐ a friend's work
COMPOSE ☐ fables **OR** ☐ folklore
PERSONIFY ☐ an animal **OR** ☐ an object
DEVELOP ☐ a tragedy **OR** ☐ a ghost story
LISTEN TO A ☐ book on tape **OR** ☐ storyteller
PLAY WITH ☐ anagrams **OR** ☐ puns
READ ABOUT ☐ sports heroes **OR** ☐ rock stars
MAKE UP ☐ similes **OR** ☐ metaphors
WRITE ☐ jokes **OR** ☐ riddles

Get inspired. Write!

Could You Be a Supreme Court Justice?

Would you be a good judge? What's true about you? I'm:

☐ good at not taking sides in an argument
☐ a good listener ☐ a hard worker ☐ fair
☐ open-minded ☐ a strong communicator
☐ passionate about the Constitution

If you checked off most of the above,
then you could be a good judge (justice).

Traditions

Quill Pens

White quills are placed on counsel tables each day that the Court sits. It's an early tradition that still remains.

Did you see the quill pens? ☐ Yes ☐ No

Handshake

All justices shake hands as they gather to enter the court. Why?

Circle one:

A. to say hello.

B. a reminder that they need to work together even if they have differences.

The justices used to wear powdered wigs.

Powdered Wigs

Thomas Jefferson said "...discard the monstrous wig which makes the English judges look like rats peeping through bunches of oakum." (Oakum is a kind of rope.) The justices have not worn them since.

The Game of Government

Pretend the government is a big soccer game. The U.S. Constitution is the rule book. There are many players in the game but there is only one referee. Who is the referee?

☐ Supreme Court ☐ President ☐ Congress
☐ Government Officials ☐ Lawyers

SUPREME COURT JUSTICE SEATING

Is there an even or odd number of Supreme Court justices?

☐ Odd ☐ Even

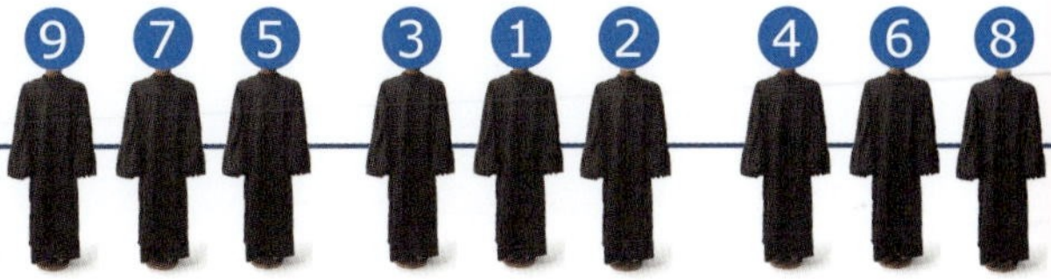

THE SUPREME COURT HAS 1 CHIEF JUSTICE AND 8 ASSOCIATE JUSTICES,

an odd number so that there will never be a tie vote. The 9 justices are seated by seniority (how long they have been on the court).

1. The Chief Justice 2. Senior Associate Justice
3. Second senior to his/her left, and so on by seniority.

OURT FIRSTS WHO'S WHO MATCHING

et a marker, draw a line nd match up the justices.

Sandra Da O'C

Louis Brandei

Roger Taney

Thurgood Marshall

Sonia Sotomayor

Antonin Scalia

1836 Fir Ca

1 Fir Jewis justice

1967 First African American ju ice

1981 First fem ju

1986 First Italian American justice

2 Fir Latina justice

SUPREME COURT

1st and East Capitol St., NE
Hours: Monday – Friday (except Federal Holi
8:30 a.m. - 4: 30 p.m.
Metro - Capitol South or Union Station
www.supremecourt.gov

President of the United States

Make a poll!

Create your own poll. Pick two items to ask about: fave museum (Natural History or Air and Space), best food in D.C. (crabs or chili), fave monument (Lincoln or Jefferson), OR whatever you want. As each person signs your book ask them which they like best. Put hatch marks below.

Declaration of Independence

(A)

United States Constitution

(B)

United States Bill of Rights

(C)

THE CHARTERS OF FREEDOM AT THE NATIONAL ARCHIVES

1. This document protects the important ideas of freedom, including the right to:
• Freedom of speech • Choose your own religion
• Assemble as a group • Have a free press

(A) (B) (C)

2. On July 4, 1776, this document told the world that the 13 British colonies of North America were leaving to form the United States of America.

(A) (B) (C)

3. In 1787, written after the War for Independence, this document created a set of rules. It is the highest law and its rules explain how the U.S. government should work.

(A) (B) (C)

IN THE ROTUNDA

What do you feel and see?
Check off what it feels like in the Rotunda.

O hot O cold O humid O dry O dark O bright

Why do you think the Rotunda is kept like this?

CHECK OUT THE HOT SPOTS

O McGowan Theater O O'Brien Gallery
O Public Vaults O Rotunda
O Bronze Doors (largest in the world).

VISIT THE PUBLIC VAULT

What were your FAVE FIVE interactive exhibits?

1.

2.

3.

4.

5.

Online visit **www.digitalvaults.org** and **www.docsteach.org**

THE NATIONAL ARCHIVES IS WHERE THE U.S. GOVERNMENT'S HISTORY IS SAVED. AN ARCHIVES IS A PLACE WHERE RECORDS ARE STORED.

WE THE PEOPLE

THE REAL STORY?

Where can YOU find the real story?

O On the Web O National Archives

Surfing the web is fun, but you have to double check what you read online. At the National Archives YOU can count on what you read and see. O True O False

At the National Archives YOU can find primary source materials (something written, recorded or used at the time and place of an event). O True O False

NARA RECORDS

Laid side to side, pages in the National Archives (NARA) would circle the Earth over 57 times!

ARCHIVE IT!

Do you have a story to tell?

O Yes O No

Document it and archive it.

What records can you save?

O Videos O Photographs

O Voicemails O Letters

O E-mails O Texts

O Tweets

NATIONAL ARCHIVES

Constitution Ave. NW [between 7th & 9th St.]
Hours: Summer 10 - 7 p.m. Winter 10 - 5:30 p.m.
Admission Free - Summer Reservations Suggested
Metro - Archives - Navy Memorial
www.archives.gov/nae

I WAS BORN IN THE TOWN OF:

I AM ____ YEARS OLD.
I HAVE ___ BROTHER(S)
AND ___ SISTER(S).

ME

____

____

MY MOM WAS BORN IN THE TOWN OF:

SHE'S ____ YEARS OLD.
SHE HAS ___ SISTER(S)
AND ___ BROTHER(S).

MY MOM

____

____

MY GRANDPARENTS MOM'S SIDE

MOM'S MOM

____

____

MOM'S DAD

____

____

MY GREAT GRANDPARENTS MOM'S SIDE

MOM'S MOM'S MOTHER

____

____

MOM'S MOM'S FATHER

____

____

MOM'S DAD'S MOTHER

____

____

MOM'S DAD'S FATHER

____

____

National Archives Genealogy

What family facts can you find at the Archives?
Did your ancestors immigrate to America? ◇Yes ◇No
Did your ancestors serve in the military? ◇ Yes ◇ No
Did your ancestors work in the government? ◇ Yes ◇ No
Were your ancestors Holocaust survivors? ◇ Yes ◇ No
Did your ancestors hold a patent? ◇ Yes ◇ No
Did your ancestors own a farm? ◇ Yes ◇ No
If you answered yes to any of these questions you can find info about your relatives at the National Archives.

My Family Archive

THE BEST THING ABOUT MY FAMILY IS:

MY DAD

____

____

MY DAD WAS BORN IN THE TOWN OF:

HE'S ____ YEARS OLD.
HE HAS ___ SISTER(S)
AND ___ BROTHER(S).

MY GRANDPARENTS DAD'S SIDE

DAD'S MOM

____

____

DAD'S DAD

____

____

MY GREAT GRANDPARENTS DAD'S SIDE

DAD'S MOM'S MOTHER

____

____

DAD'S DAD'S FATHER

____

____

DAD'S DAD'S MOTHER

____

____

DAD'S DAD'S FATHER

____

____

Start a Family History

Are you a good detective? ◇Yes ◇No
The oldest person in my family is ___________
Can you interview that person? ◇Yes ◇No
Can you gather family photographs? ◇Yes ◇No
Can you find the birth date for each person in your family and research what major events happened that year and every ten years after? ◇Yes ◇No
Can you fit your family into history? ◇Yes ◇No
Did you find info at the National Archives?◇Yes ◇No

At the White House Spot Marine One

Marine One is the president's transport for short trips. What is Marine One?

O Limo O Boat O Helicopter

Hint: Marine One can fly in groups and move around so no one knows the secret location of the president.

Protecting the President

In the picture above, who is standing on the White House roof?

O Tourists O Secret Service O Reporters

If you guessed the Secret Service you are right. They protect the president and are divided into two groups:

O Special Agents

O Uniformed Officers

Can you spot both at the White House? Check them off if you see them.

Spot the White House Visitor Center

@ 1450 Pennsylvania Avenue, N.W.
Did you know, the White House sits on President's Park, which has been a national park since 1933?

How many gallons of white paint does it take to paint the outside of the White House? ○ 105 ○ 257 ○ 570

Who was the first president to live in the White House?
○ Washington ○ Adams ○ Jefferson

Did you get your Junior Ranger Badge? ○ Yes ○ No

Who was the tallest president?
○ Lincoln ○ Washington ○ Jefferson ○ Kennedy

What is the name of the president's office?
○ West Wing ○ The Oval Office ○ East Wing

WE THE PEOPLE

Can I tour the White House?

You CAN tour the White House, but you have to request a tour from your member of Congress. Who is your member of Congress?

____

Call 202-456-7041 to find out more.
Call the Congressional operator 202-224-3121.
Did you tour the White House? O Yes O No

The Presidential Seal

Until 1959, 48 stars circled the eagle. Now, how many are there?

____

The eagle has not faced the arrows since WWII.

The olive branch symbolizes peace.

The 13 arrows symbolize the 13 original colonies.

The seal is used as a symbol of the president on vehicles, podiums and documents.

White House

1600 Pennsylvania Avenue, NW
Admission Free - Reservations Required
For more information call 202-456-7041
Metro - McPherson Square or Farragut West
www.whitehouse.gov

If You Could...

be the president, what is the first thing you would change?

Your Space

Write your ideas, doodle or be deep and serious! This is your space. You make the RULES!

White House Pets

1. Who was the last president to keep a cow on the White House lawn? ◇ Lincoln ◇ Taft ◇ Bush
2. What giant pachyderm was given to President Eisenhower? ◇ Rhino ◇ Hippo ◇ Elephant
3. What animals did China give to President Nixon? ◇ 2 Giant Pandas ◇ 2 Elephants ◇ 2 Alligators
4. In 1918, what animals helped mow the White House lawn? ◇ Goats ◇ Sheep ◇ Cows
5. Our 6th president, John Quincy Adams, was given what unusual animal as a gift? ◇ Snake ◇ Lizard ◇ Alligator
6. Lincoln's sons Tad and Willie had two goats, Nanny and Nanko, who ran wild in the White House. ◇ Myth ◇ Fact

Find out more at the White House Visitors Center

---

1. Taft's cow Pauline was a dairy cow and gave the White House fresh milk. 2. A baby elephant called Dzimbo arrived at the White House from Africa, and was given a home at the National Zoo. 3. Two Giant Pandas, Ling- Ling and Hsing- Hsing, were given to the White House and were the first pandas to live at the National Zoo. 4. A flock of sheep grazed the White House grounds and their wool was donated to the Red Cross. 5. The Marquis de Lafayette gave a Chinese alligator to Adams. It lived in the White House until Adams left office. 6. Fact. Tad and Willie would hitch the goats up to chairs and have them pull them through the White House.

Counterfeit Money

What if you get counterfeit money?

- Counterfeit money is not real money.
- You can't go to a bank and change counterfeit money into real money.
- It is illegal to knowingly use counterfeit money.
- Learn to spot it, so you don't get stuck with it.

Make Sure It's Not Counterfeit

Security Thread
Hold the bill up to the light and look for the plastic strip in the paper. It runs up and down one side of the note. Look closely; what do you see?

Color Shifting Ink
Look at the number "20." When you tilt the note up and down the ink changes color from copper to green.

Serial Numbers
Twice on the front of every note you will find 11 letters and numbers. Can you find both? They help the police and Secret Service find counterfeit notes.

Watermark
Hold the bill up to the light and look for the faint image or watermark. Look closely; what do you see there?

To Serve and Protect

This law enforcement group not only protects the president but is also responsible for catching counterfeiters.

S _ C R _ T S _ R V _ C _

Secret Service

My Fave Five

1.
2.
3.
4.
5.

WHO'S ON THE BILL?

Match the money to the man.

Andrew Jackson on the front and the White House on the back.

Benjamin Franklin on the front and Independence Hall on the back.

Ulysses S. Grant on the front and the U.S. Capitol on the back.

Abraham Lincoln on the front and the Lincoln Memorial on the back.

Alexander Hamilton on the front and the U.S. Treasury on the back.

WE THE PEOPLE

MY MAD MONEY

If money grew on trees how would you spend it? ______________________

____

____

What are some ways that you would make money?

- Dog Walking
- Yard Work
- Babysitting

How much do you get for allowance?

- $2
- $5
- $10
- ______

Are you good with your money?

- Yes
- No

What do you do with your money?

- Put it in the bank
- Spend it
- Invest it

When you earn money where do you put it?

- Wallet
- Sock Drawer
- Piggy Bank
- Bank

Money match: 5 Lincoln, 10 Hamilton, 20 Jackson, 50 Grant, 100 Franklin

BUREAU OF ENGRAVING

14th and C Streets, S.W.
Winter - Mon- Fri 8:30 a.m. - 3:30 p.m.
Summer - Mon- Fri 8:30 a.m. - 7:30 p.m. (tickets)
In the summer free same-day tickets are offered at 8 a.m. They go quickly, usually by 9 a.m. For more ticket info go to www.moneyfactory.gov

If You Could...

have all the money that prints in one day at the Bureau of Engraving (around 38 million notes–worth about 750 million dollars), what would you do with it?

Your Space

This is your space. You make the rules! Write, doodle or daydream about how you would use your money.

Who am I? I am Alexander Hamilton, a founding father and the first Secretary of the Treasury.

If I had all the money that the Bureau of Engraving prints in 1 day,

I would rather...

- ☐ save it **OR** ☐ spend it
- ☐ invest in stocks **OR** ☐ put it in a bank
- ☐ donate to charity **OR** ☐ start a charity
- ☐ buy a mansion **OR** ☐ help the homeless
- ☐ travel the world **OR** ☐ start a business
- ☐ start my college fund **OR** ☐ give scholarships
- ☐ save the animals **OR** ☐ buy a rainforest
- ☐ help the homeless **OR** ☐ save a species
- ☐ work to stop wars **OR** ☐ feed the hungry
- ☐ build a pool **OR** ☐ build a community pool
- ☐ save the whales **OR** ☐ build solar farms
- ☐ ________________ **OR** ☐ ________________
- ☐ ________________ **OR** ☐ ________________

Poll your friends and family. See what they think.

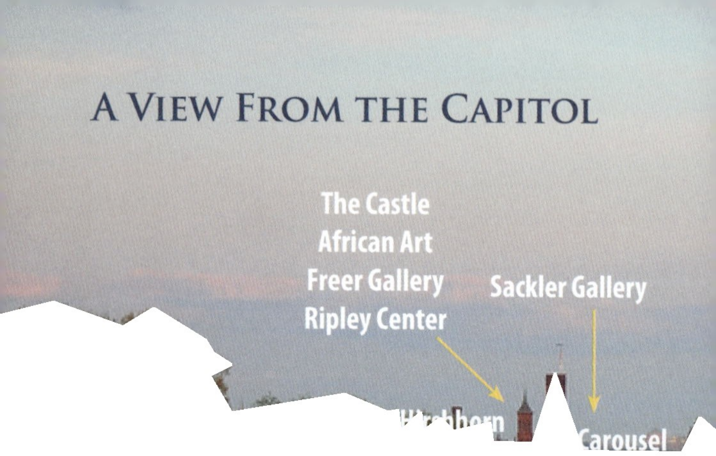

CHECK IT OUT. CHECK IT OFF. RATE IT!

Find each sight on MY MAPS pages 10-13

NATIONAL MALL EAST

- ☐ **United States Capitol** ☆ ☆ ☆ ☆ ☆
- ☐ **Ulysses S. Grant Memorial** ☆ ☆ ☆ ☆ ☆
- ☐ **US Botanical Gardens** ☆ ☆ ☆ ☆ ☆
- ☐ **American Indian Museum** ☆ ☆ ☆ ☆ ☆
- ☐ **Air and Space Museum** ☆ ☆ ☆ ☆ ☆
- ☐ **Hirshhorn Museum** ☆ ☆ ☆ ☆ ☆
- ☐ **Hirshhorn Sculpture Garden** ☆ ☆ ☆ ☆ ☆
- ☐ **Arts and Industries Building (closed)**
- ☐ **Carousel on the Mall** ☆ ☆ ☆ ☆ ☆
- ☐ **Smithsonian Castle & Garden** ☆ ☆ ☆ ☆ ☆
- ☐ **Ripley Cnt/Discovery Theater** ☆ ☆ ☆ ☆ ☆
- ☐ **Museum of African Art** ☆ ☆ ☆ ☆ ☆
- ☐ **Freer Gallery of Art** ☆ ☆ ☆ ☆ ☆
- ☐ **Arthur M. Sackler Gallery** ☆ ☆ ☆ ☆ ☆
- ☐ **Washington Monument** ☆ ☆ ☆ ☆ ☆
- ☐ **Museum of American History** ☆ ☆ ☆ ☆ ☆
- ☐ **Museum of Natural History** ☆ ☆ ☆ ☆ ☆
- ☐ **National Gallery Sculpture Garden** ☆ ☆ ☆ ☆ ☆
- ☐ **National Gallery of Art** ☆ ☆ ☆ ☆ ☆

NATIONAL MALL WEST

- ☐ **World War II Memorial** ☆ ☆ ☆ ☆ ☆
- ☐ **Reflecting Pool** ☆ ☆ ☆ ☆ ☆
- ☐ **Constitution Gardens** ☆ ☆ ☆ ☆ ☆
- ☐ **Vietnam Veterans Memorial** ☆ ☆ ☆ ☆ ☆
- ☐ **Lincoln Memorial** ☆ ☆ ☆ ☆ ☆
- ☐ **Korean War Veterans Memorial** ☆ ☆ ☆ ☆ ☆
- ☐ **D.C. War Memorial** ☆ ☆ ☆ ☆ ☆

MY FAVE FIVE ON THE MALL

1.
2.
3.
4.
5.

How many miles is it from the U.S. Capitol to the Lincoln Memorial?

☐ half a mile ☐ one mile ☐ two miles

Walking quickly, how many minutes would it take you to walk from the U.S. Capitol to the Lincoln Memorial?

☐ 10 ☐ 30 ☐ 60

Answers: 2 miles, about 30 minutes

NATIONAL MALL

The National Mall starts at the foot of the U.S. Capitol at 1st St. It ends just after 23rd St and the Lincoln Memorial.
Metro - Smithsonian & L'Enfant Plaza
www.nps.gov/mall

National Park Service

Washington Monument Fact ◄◄

World War II Memorial Fact ►►

Lincoln Memorial Fact ◄◄

Korean War Veterans Memorial Fact ►►

Vietnam Veterans Memorial Fact ◄◄

E-mail us your fave facts and we'll post them on our website: info@AllAboutMEinDC.com

Ranger Fun Facts

For each memorial and monument write your fave fact.

Can you spot rangers on the National Mall? Ask the rangers "What's your favorite fact?"

MONUMENTS

Tidal Basin and Japanese Cherry Tree ◄◄ Fact

Thomas Jefferson Memorial Fact ►►

Franklin Delano Roosevelt Memorial ◄◄ Fact

Martin Luther King Jr. Memorial Fact ►►

Upload your photos, stories and fave facts at: www.AllAboutMEinDC.com

TAKE THE STAIRS

Were you one of the lucky ones that walked down the steps? How many steps are there?

◇ 555 ◇ 896 ◇ 1100

MEMORIAL STONES

On the walk down did you see memorial stones? How many stones are there?

◇ 13 ◇ 50 ◇ 193

Answer:
896 steps
193 stones

How is the monument held together?

Gravity. The weight of the stone holds it together. It can withstand tornado force winds.

In 1876, when they restarted construction, the first quarry had run out of stone. They had to use stone from a new quarry. It was a different color.

Can you see two colors?

Stopped construction. They ran out of money.

Building Restarted: 1876

Building stopped 150 feet: 1854

Building Began in 1848

How many flags surround the monument?

○ 50 ○ 36 ○ 13

50 flags surround the monument, representing the 50 states. Combined, can you calculate how many stars are on the flags?

In Virginia, did you visit George Washington's home, Mount Vernon?
◇ Yes ◇ No

ASK A RANGER

In 1884, how did they get the capstone to the top? It weighs 3,300 pounds!

Hi, I'm George, the first and only president in U.S. history to be elected unanimously. In 1789, how many states were there?
◇ 50 ◇ 36 ◇ 13

In the new elevator, how long does it take to get to the top?
◇ 3 minutes ◇ 1 minute ◇ 70 seconds

The first elevator was steam powered, open sided and took 12 long minutes to the top. Some say women were banned from riding in it.
◇ Myth? ◇ Fact?

13 states, 70 seconds, Myth.

For about 20 years construction stopped.

Fast Facts

- ★A monument to our first president.
- ★555' 5⅛" tall.
- ★Tallest building in D.C.
- ★An obelisk: a 4-sided pillar with a pyramid atop.

Washington Monument

Open every day but July 4th and Christmas
Free - tickets required - www.nps.gov/wamo
In advance reserve tickets at www.recreation.gov or get same-day tickets at the Washington Monument Lodge on 15th St. at 8:30 a.m.

IS THERE ANYTHING YOU
FEEL STRONGLY ABOUT?
WHAT IS IT?
IS IT WORTH STANDING UP FOR?

Would you have been a PATRIOT, a LOYALIST or NEUTRAL?

In 1775, when the War for Independence began, I was asked to command the Continental Army. I chose to be a **Patriot**. I fought against the British Redcoats, Loyalists and King George III for American Independence.

Which side would you take?

- ◇ PATRIOT
- ◇ LOYALIST
- ◇ NEUTRAL

Patriots were against taxation without representation. **Loyalists** were loyal to King George III and England. **Neutralists** couldn't make up their minds and were sometimes called fence sitters.

Patriots were courageous, but could have been put in prison or hung for treason.

Some people say that the back of my head is sculpted to look like General Lee looking sadly toward to his old Virginia home.
◇ Myth ◇ Fact

I, Abraham Lincoln, am buried underneath, or entombed within, the stone structure of the Lincoln Memorial
◇ Myth ◇ Fact

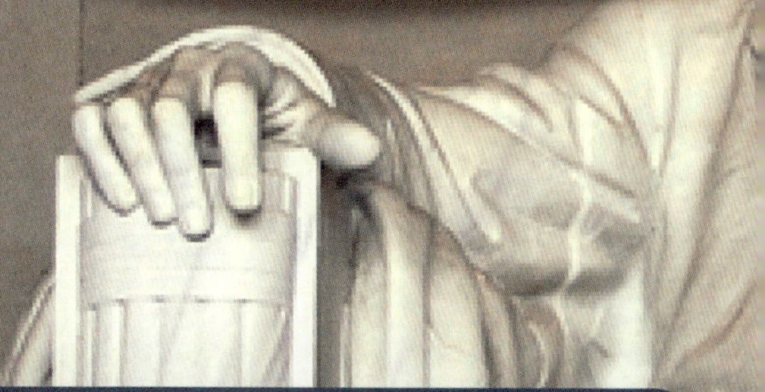

Fast Facts

Temple of Zeus. The Lincoln Memorial was inspired by ancient Greek temples.

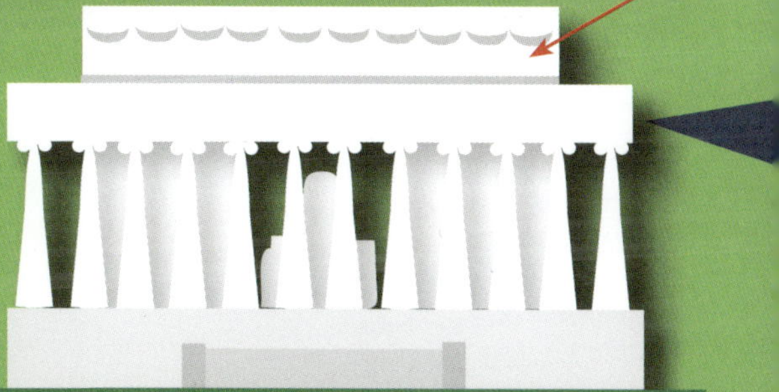

Potomac River The Lincoln Memorial was built where the Potomac River once ran.

Can you Spot it?

Columns
36 around the outside. One for each state in the Union the year Lincoln died.

Euture
In the 2nd Inaugural Address, FUTURE was first engraved starting with the letter E.

57 Steps
Do the 57 steps have meaning? No. Lincoln died when he was 56, not 57.

Paste Fave Photo Here

Have fun and think creatively.
What great shots can you take
at the monuments?

(Be respectful)

Paste your
favorite photo
of yourself on the
National Mall
in Washington, D.C.

Don't forget to turn your camera
and shoot a vertical portrait.
Print size:
3 X 5

MONUMENTAL MOMENTS

Write in YOUR own quotes above. Take YOUR own photos.

Paste Funny Photo Here

Idea:
At the Lincoln Memorial,
put out your hand and pretend
you are holding the
Washington Monument in midair.
Or
Put your finger at the top
of the monument so it looks like
you are touching the top.

Have a friend take the
picture. They'll have to position it
just right so the illusion works.

Don't forget to turn your camera
and shoot a vertical portrait.
Print size:
3 X 5

Would you have been a PATRIOT, a LOYALIST or NEUTRAL?

Circle A, B or C

Are you afraid to try new things?
A Yes B No C I don't know!

Do you like to follow the rules?
A Yes B No C I don't know!

Do you believe it is important to be fair?
A No B Yes C I don't know!

Do you like a challenge?
A No B Yes C I don't know!

If you circled mostly :
A's - you might be a LOYALIST
B's - you might be a PATRIOT
C's - you might be NEUTRAL

Answers left page: Myth, Myth. Right page: Fact, Myth.

Engraved **on top** are the **48 states** in the U.S. when the memorial was finished.

Alaska and Hawaii became states after the memorial was finished. Can you find the marker?

Engraved **above the columns** are the **36 States** in the U.S. when Lincoln died.

He reunited the 25 northern **Union States** and 11 southern **Confederate States** but died before the wounds of war could heal.

April 9, 1865 - General Lee surrenders.

April 14, 1865 - Lincoln is assassinated.

Lincoln Memorial

National Mall (23rd Street N.W.)
Open 24 hours. No tickets needed.
Rangers are on duty daily: 9:30 a.m. to 11:30 p.m.
Don't miss the ranger talks.
www.nps.gov/linc

If You Could...

go back in time and meet any famous American who would it be? Why?

Your Space

Listen to the ranger talks at my memorial. Jot down your thoughts, take a poll or use this as a seat. This is your space.

Abe & Animals

1. As a lawyer, Abe rode to courthouses all around Illinois. What two baby animals did he rescue in a windstorm?
◇ Two baby birds ◇ Two fawns ◇ Two goslings
2. At the White House, what two pets named Nanny and Nanko would come to the President's side when he called?
◇ 2 dogs ◇ 2 cats ◇ 2 goats
3. On Christmas Eve, Abe's son Tad asked that this animal be given a stay of execution. It was saved and given a presidential "order of reprieve."
◇ A turkey ◇ A goose ◇ A pheasant
4. What pets did Lincoln leave in Springfield for fear that the trip was too long to Washington?
◇ Fido the dog ◇ Bob the horse ◇ All of the above
5. Three weeks before the Civil War ended, Abe rescued which orphaned animals at General Grant's headquarters?
◇ 3 kittens ◇ 2 puppies ◇ 2 baby chicks

---

1. Two baby birds had been blown from their nest. He refused to ride on until he found their mother. 2.Two goats, which sometimes slept with Lincoln's sons. Willie and Tad could be seen whizzing through the White House on a goat-pulled chair. 3. A turkey, which became Tad's pet, Jack. Jack followed Tad all around the White House grounds. 4 Bob and Fido. At Abe's funeral Bob wore a mourning blanket and Fido was at the house with the family. 5. Three kittens. He said to them, "Kitties, thank God you are cats, and can't understand this terrible war that is going on."

Hi, I'm
Thomas Jefferson.
I was one of the
authors of this document:
_ _ C L _ R _ T _ _ N
OF
_ N D _ P _ N D _ N C _

I was Vice
President under
J _ H N _ D _ M S
And the
T H _ R _
President of the
United States.

From France and
Napoleon I bought the
territory of Louisiana.
The deal was called the
L _ _ _ S _ _ N _ P _ R C H _ S _

Who did I send to
explore the west?
L _ W _ S & C L _ R _

I believed that
all men have a right
to an education.
So I created the
_ N _ V _ R S _ T _
_ F
V _ R G _ N _ A.

John Adams and I
died on this same day:
July __, 1826,
the 50th anniversary of
America's
Independence.

Answers left page:
Declaration of Independence.
John Adams, Third,
Louisiana Purchase,
Lewis and Clark, University
of Virginia, July 4.
Answers right page:
Pediment , Jefferson is
in the middle, Metal
shortage, plaster.

Can you spot...

...a triangular space above the columns? What is this called? P ■ D ■ M ■ N T

This is where you can spot the 5 men who wrote the Declaration of Independence. Which one do YOU think is Jefferson?

Can you spot...

...a bronze statue of Thomas Jefferson? In 1943, why did the memorial open without the bronze statue? ■ The statue was lost. ■ Metal shortages during WWII.

A temporary P L ■ S T ■ R statue was made and painted to look like bronze.

MONUMENTS

JEFFERSON MEMORIAL

Tidal Basin - 900 Ohio Drive, SW
Free - Open 24 hours a day -
Rangers are on duty from 9:30 a.m. to 11:30 p.m.
Metro - Smithsonian
www.nps.gov/thje

If You Could...
change one thing about American history, what would it be?

The other side of Jefferson
SLAVERY

Although Jefferson wrote that "all men are created equal," he owned slaves. ☐ True ☐ False

He spoke against slavery in the Declaration of Independence, but the wording was taken out. ☐ True ☐ False

He passed a bill to ban the import of slaves from Africa to Virginia. ☐ True ☐ False

Jefferson died and owed a lot of money. ☐ True ☐ False

After his funeral, 130 of his slaves were auctioned off to pay his debts. ☐ True ☐ False

All the statements above are true.

Wow, this guy was incredible!

The Declaration of Independence is at the top of the list, but Thomas Jefferson had an amazing life.

What do YOU know about Jefferson?

Thomas Jefferson was governor of what state?
☐ Pennsylvania ☐ Virginia ☐ Massachusetts

Who did Jefferson replace as Minister of France?
☐ John Adams ☐ Benjamin Franklin

For what president was he the 1st U.S. Secretary of State?
☐ John Adams ☐ George Washington

Thomas Jefferson was our 3rd president and the first to shake hands rather than bow. ☐ true ☐ false

What small sum did Jefferson pay Napoleon and France for the entire Louisiana Territory (the Louisiana Purchase)?
☐ 150 million ☐ 15 million

What animal did Lewis and Clark and explorer Zebulon Pike send back to Jefferson in the White House? ☐ Magpies ☐ Prairie dog ☐ 2 grizzly bears ☐ All of the above

Thomas Jefferson designed this home in Virginia.
☐ Monticello ☐ Mount Vernon ☐ Montpelier

Virginia, Franklin, Washington, true, 15 million, All of the above, Monticello

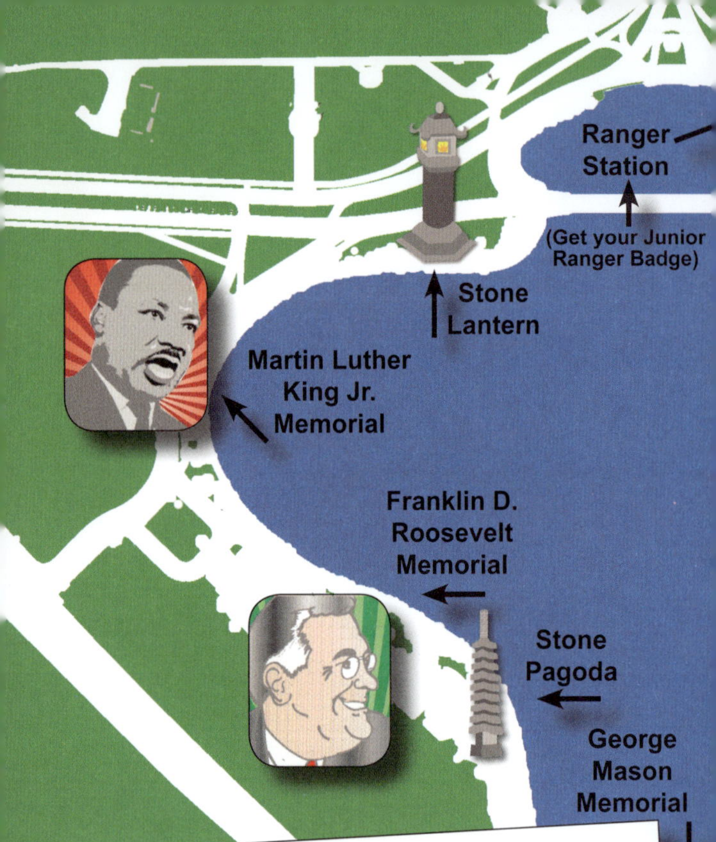

Japanese Cherry Trees

They surround the Tidal Basin. In 1912, how many trees were sent to Washington from Tokyo, Japan?

O 100 O 2,005 O 3,020

Japanese Stone Lantern

This 350-year-old lantern is the oldest stone sculpture in D.C. It is lit each spring during the cherry blossom festival and has a twin in Japan.

O Myth O Fact

Japanese Stone Pagoda

Given to D.C. from Japan after World War II, it came in pieces like a puzzle with no instructions.

O Myth O Fact

Franklin D. Roosevelt Memorial

The memorial has 4 outdoor rooms, 1 for each of his terms as president. How many terms was he elected?

O 1 O 2 O 3 O 4

Martin Luther King Jr. Memorial

Dr. King worked to make America a place where all men are treated equally. At the Lincoln Memorial what famous speech did Dr. King give?

O Declaration of Independence O I Have a Dream

George Mason Memorial

George Mason refused to sign what document because it did not speak out against slavery?

O Declaration of Independence O Constitution

Answers: 3,020. Fact. Fact. 4. I Have a Dream. Constitution

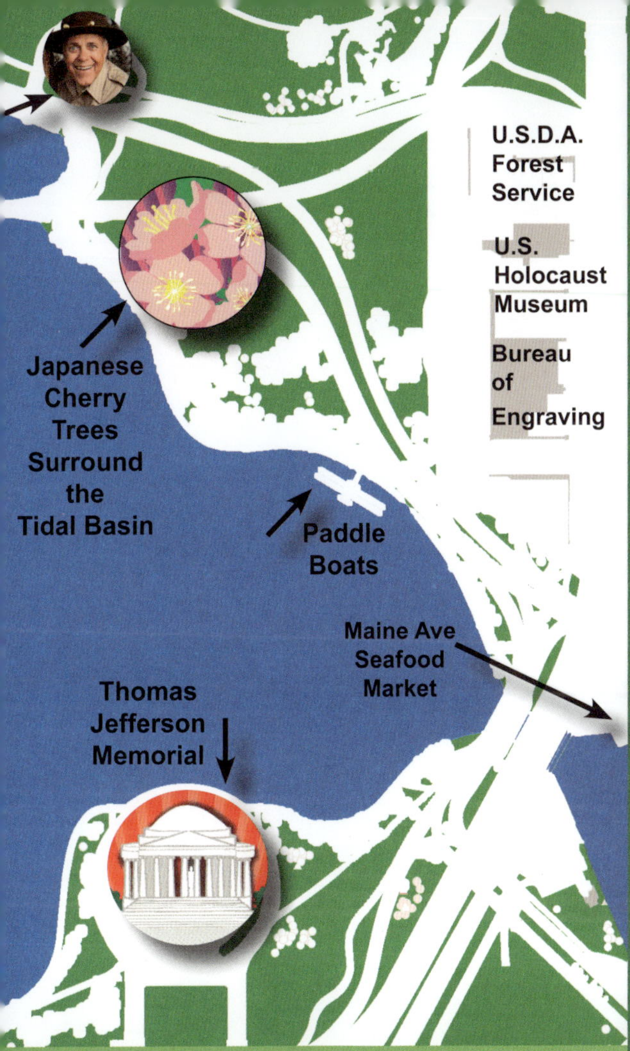

MY FAVE FIVE @ THE TIDAL BASIN

1.
2.
3.
4.
5.

TIDAL BASIN

South of the Washington Monument. Bordered by Independence Ave, Raoul Wallenberg Place.
Open 24 hours a day.
Rangers 9:30 a.m. - 11:30 p.m.
Metro - Smithsonian - www.nps.gov

MONUMENTS

Your Space - Doodle, write or paste photos.

Cherry Blossom Trivia

What do YOU know?

When were the 3020 cherry trees given to Washington from Tokyo, Japan?

O 1910 O 1912 O 1945

By steamship, they traveled across the Pacific only to be faced with the 2000-mile trip across America by train. It is amazing that they arrived alive and well. How long was the trip?

O 10 days O 25 days O 40 days

The 3020 trees were not the first trees given to D.C. In 1910, the Japanese sent 2000 trees but sadly they didn't do well on the trip and had to be burned. Why?

O They were older trees O They became sick

O Insects infested the trees O All of the above

Where are most of the cherry trees planted?

O Tidal Basin O White House O U.S. Capitol

Which came first?

O The Jefferson Memorial O The Cherry Trees

In D.C., about when do the cherry trees bloom?

O March 25 - April 4 O May 1 -15 O June 10 - 24

Did you see the cherry trees in bloom? O Yes O No

Did you do the Junior Ranger program? O Yes O No

1912 • 40 Days • All of the above • Tidal Basin
• The Cherry Trees came first • Around March 25 - April 4

What a View

After Martha died, our grandson inherited the land for Arlington House. He built a house high on the hill overlooking the capital and turned it into a museum dedicated to me.

The following had not been built yet:

★ Memorial Bridge ★ Lincoln Memorial
★ Washington Monument

Can you imagine the view?

☐ Yes ☐ No

My Great Grand Daughter

My grandson had one child that lived to be an adult. Her name was Mary Custis. She married Robert E. Lee, and they lived together at Arlington House (Lee-Custis Mansion).

63 VIPs

There would be no Arlington House without the 63 people who built, lived and worked there. Visit the Slave Quarters Museum.

Can you find the stories of:

- ☐ Jim Parks, buried at Arlington
- ☐ George Clark, the plantation cook
- ☐ Selina Gray, Mrs. Lee's trusted maid

Lee Left Arlington

I asked General Lee to command the Union Army during the Civil War. Lee said no. He felt that he needed to follow his home state of Virginia. He resigned the Union Army and joined the Confederacy. Lee left Arlington House for Richmond and never returned.

☐ Myth ☐ Fact

If you were General Lee what would you do?

- ☐ Join the Confederacy and his home state Virginia.
- ☐ Command the Union Army and leave Virginia.

Union StrongHold

After Generel Lee left, why did the Union Army take over Arlington House and its grounds?

- ☐ To defend the capital
- ☐ For soldier barracks
- ☐ All of the Above

Cemetery

Sadly, many soldiers died in the Civil War and there was no space to bury them. Some say Union General Meigs buried soldiers in Lee's front yard to get even for Lee leaving the Union Army.

■ True ■ False

Now Arlington is the resting place for over 300,000 people, and there are about 100 funerals a week.

Junior Ranger

At Arlington House, did you do the Junior Ranger program? ■ Yes ■ No

The eternal Flame

President John F. Kennedy was assassinated on November 22, 1963. He was buried at Arlington Cemetery. Who lit the eternal flame at JFK's funeral/gravesite?

■ Jackie Kennedy ■ President Lyndon B. Johnson

Tomb of the Unknowns

How many steps does the Honor Guard take during his walk across the Tomb of the Unknowns? Why? Hint: it symbolizes the honored military gun salute.

■ 3 ■ 7 ■ 21

Left page answers: Fact, Lee never returned. All of the above. Right page: False (no written record), Jackie Kennedy, 21 steps

Arlington Cemetery

Arlington National Cemetery and the Robert. E. Lee Memorial (Arlington House)
Hours 8 a.m. - 7 p.m., Oct-Mar 8 a.m. - 5 p.m.
Admission Free - Tourmobile recommended
Metro - Arlington Cemetery

If You Could...

pick one person in history and ask them a question to which they had to give a truthful answer who would you pick, and what question would you ask?

Your Space

Write your ideas, doodle or be deep and serious! This is your space. You make the rules!

Who am I? I am General Robert E. Lee, commander of the Confederate Army.

Would you have lived in Confederate or Union Territory?

Do you live in the United States? ☐ Yes ☐ No
If yes, in the paragraphs below **find your state** and circle it. Were you in Confederate or Union territory? Maybe your state was not a state yet?

☐ **Confederate** (11 Southern states)
Did you know... By 1861, 11 states out of 36 states left to form their own government. It was called the Confederacy. **South Carolina** was the first state to secede in 1860 and asked the other slave-holding states to join in forming a new nation. By February 1861 six other states followed. They were **Mississippi, Florida, Alabama, Georgia, Louisiana, and Texas.** Next, **Virginia** seceded. Finally, **North Carolina, Tennessee,** and **Arkansas** joined.

☐ **Union** (25 Northern States)
25 states stayed in the Union including the slave states of **Missouri, Kentucky, Maryland,** and **Delaware. Western Virginia split from Virginia forming the new free state of West Virginia.** Twenty more states remained in the Union including: **California, Connecticut, Illinois, Indiana, Iowa, Kansas, Maine, Massachusetts, Michigan, Minnesota, Nevada, New Hampshire, New York, New Jersey, Ohio, Oregon, Pennsylvania, Rhode Island, Vermont, Wisconsin. Washington, D.C**. was Union territory but it is not a state now and was not a state then.

☐ **Not Yet States** (14 states)
The following became states after the Civil War ended: **Nebraska, Colorado, North Dakota, South Dakota, Montana, Washington, Idaho, Wyoming, Utah, Oklahoma, New Mexico, Arizona, Alaska and Hawaii.**

SPY MUSEUM

IDENTITY

You need to create a new identity.
What nationality would you choose?

- ☐ Another American - I'm not a very good actor.
- ☐ Australian - I can do the accent.
- ☐ Russian - I'm the silent type.

SPY GADGETS

What is your gadget of choice?

- ☐ Spy Alarm - motion detector
- ☐ Spy Sunglasses – video camera
- ☐ Spy Watch - Two-way walkie talkies

OPERATION UNDERCOVER

How would you disguise yourself? Can you trick your friends?

HAIR

- ☐ Cover up
- ☐ Dye
- ☐ Curl
- ☐ Straighten
- ☐ Wig

CLOTHES

- ☐ Elevator shoes
- ☐ Trench coat
- ☐ Scarf
- ☐ Uniform
- ☐ Hat

FACE

- Sunglasses ☐
- Eye color ☐
- Make up ☐
- Eyebrows ☐
- Eye patch ☐
- Mustache ☐

SPEECH

- A foreign accent ☐
- Local accent ☐
- Pitch ☐
- Mumble ☐

POSTURE AND LOOK

☐ Slouch ☐ Stand tall
☐ *Limp ☐ Skin color

Tip * to remember to walk differently - put a pebble or penny in your shoe.

ENCRYPTION

BREAK THE CODE

A	B	C	D	E	F	G	H	I	J	K	L	M
►	▲	▫	≈	◄	♥	♠	•	Ω	♦	ψ	‼	≥

N	O	P	Q	R	S	T	U	V	W	X	Y	Z
≤	⌐	╨	△	φ	Џ	♪	▼	≠	€	£	›	д

▫ ⌐ ≈ ◄ ▲ φ ◄ ► ψ ◄ φ

Create your own message.

code breaker

YOUR MISSION, SHOULD YOU CHOOSE TO ACCEPT IT: SPY ON THE SPY MUSEUM. BE OBSERVANT, GATHER INTELLIGENCE.

FAVE 5 SPY GADGETS

1.

2.

3.

4.

5.

ARE YOU READY?

Kids 12 and up, are you ready for a live action spy adventure? ☐ Yes ☐ No

For this one-hour adrenaline-fueled mission, you are the spy. You have to locate a missing nuclear trigger before it ends up in the wrong hands. Have you ever: Cracked a safe? ☐ Yes ☐ No

Decoded secret messages? ☐ Yes ☐ No

Interrogated a double agent? ☐ Yes ☐ No

Worked under pressure? ☐ Yes ☐ No

Are you ready to be a spy? ☐ Yes ☐ No

No spy experience necessary.

operation SPY™

INTERNATIONAL SPY MUSEUM

800 F Street, NW
Hours and Admission rates vary
For more info go to www.spymuseum.org
Metro - Gallery Place/Chinatown

YOUR SPACE

Make a secret code, doodle or write a spy thriller!

This is your space. You make the rules!

DOUBLE AGENT

Are you good at :

- Deception
- Keeping secrets
- Trickery
- Faking Loyalty
- Betrayal

NINJA

Are you good at :

- Martial Arts
- Scaling Walls
- Creeping Quietly
- Picking Locks
- Being Sneaky

SECRET AGENT

Are you:

- Loyal
- Patriotic
- Creative
- Trustworthy
- Intelligent

Which would you be?

- Ninja
- Double Agent
- Secret Agent

INTERNATIONAL
SPY
MUSEUM
WASHINGTON DC

Newseum - Don't miss

Check it off as you visit each exhibit:

☐ *What's News* Film ☐ Berlin Wall
☐ The Comics ☐ Today's Front Page
☐ News History Gallery ☐ Be a TV Reporter
☐ Newsroom & Ethics Table ☐ 4D Film
☐ 6th Floor Terrace on Pennsylvania Avenue

World News

Why is freedom of speech so important? Do all countries have this freedom?

O Yes O No

How would you feel if you lived in a country that didn't allow you to say what you want?

O Calm O Angry O Irritated O Frustrated

The 1st Amendment Gallery

In the First Amendment of the U.S. Constitution there are 5 rights. Which are important for journalists?

Freedom of:

☐ Religion ☐ Speech ☐ the Press
☐ Petition ☐ Assembly

I-Witness

Did you shake, rattle, and roll and experience this 4D film?

O Yes O No

The Newseum has fifteen theatres. How many films did you see? ______

My Fave Five at Newseum

1.

2.

Reporter Skills

Could you be a reporter? Check your character traits:

☐ Curious ☐ A people person ☐ A hard worker
☐ Courageous ☐ A human lie detector
☐ Skilled at getting answers ☐ A good listener
☐ A writer ☐ A good researcher

My NEWS

What kind of journalist would you be?
● TV ● Print ● Internet ● Radio ● Film

If you were a foreign correspondent where would you go?
● Europe ● Asia ● Africa ● S. America ● Australia

Do you read a newspaper every day? ● Yes ● No

Where do you get your news?
● Internet ● Television ● Newspaper ● Radio

If you were a journalist what would you write about?
● Sports ● Business ● Health ● Politics

NEWSEUM

Be a Photographer or a Camera Person

On level 2, in the NBC News Interactive Newsroom, use the touch-screen stations to see if you have what it takes to be a photographer. Which would you rather be?

☐ Camera Person

☐ Photographer

Newseum

555 Pennsylvania Ave., NW
Hours 9 a.m. to 5 p.m. daily. Closed Thanksgiving, Christmas and New Year's Day.
Admission Rates - Go to www.Newseum.org
Metro - Archives/Navy Memorial-Penn Quarter

Extra! Extra!

If you could tell the world a news story what would the headline be? Write your story.

Cut out a picture of your face.

Paste it here.

Read all about it!

What medium would you use to tell your story?

O Photography O Video O Print O Internet

Be a Reporter

At the Newseum on level 2, there are eight "Be a Reporter" stations where you can pick up a microphone, step before a camera and experience what it takes to be a TV reporter.

Do you have what it takes to be a TV reporter?

OYes ONo

Do you get nervous in front of a camera?

OYes ONo

Is it hard for you to read a teleprompter?

OYes ONo

Top Ten Gardens

Check off the gardens as you visit them. Rate each. Give them one star, five stars, or somewhere in between.

National Mall

- ☐ US Botanic Gardens ☆ ☆ ☆ ☆ ☆
  100 Maryland Avenue, SW. - National Mall www.usbg.gov
- ☐ National Gallery Sculpture Garden ☆ ☆ ☆ ☆ ☆
  National Mall at 7th Street and Constitution
  www.nga.gov/exhibitions/sculptureinfo.shtm
- ☐ Smithsonian Gardens - National Mall
  www.gardens.si.edu/horticulture/gardens1.htm
  - ☐ Enid A. Haupt Garden - the Castle ☆ ☆ ☆ ☆ ☆
  - ☐ Ripley Garden - Arts and Industries ☆ ☆ ☆ ☆ ☆
  - ☐ Hirshhorn Sculpture Garden ☆ ☆ ☆ ☆ ☆
  - ☐ Native Landscape - American Indian ☆ ☆ ☆ ☆ ☆
  - ☐ Butterfly Habitat - Natural History ☆ ☆ ☆ ☆ ☆
- ☐ Constitution Gardens ☆ ☆ ☆ ☆ ☆
  Constitution Avenue and 17th Street, NW - National Mall
  www.nps.gov/coga

Georgetown and Uptown

- ☐ Dumbarton Oaks ☆ ☆ ☆ ☆ ☆
  1703 32nd Street, NW - Upper Georgetown
  www.doaks.org/gardens
- ☐ C&O Canal ☆ ☆ ☆ ☆ ☆
  1057 Thomas Jefferson Street, NW - Lower Georgetown
  www.nps.gov/choh
- ☐ National Cathedral Gardens ☆ ☆ ☆ ☆ ☆
  3101 Wisconsin Ave, N.W. www.nationalcathedral.org
- ☐ Hillwood Museum and Gardens ☆ ☆ ☆ ☆ ☆
  4155 Linnean Avenue, NW - 1 mile from National Zoo
  www.hillwoodmuseum.org

New York Avenue and Beyond

- ☐ National Arboretum ☆ ☆ ☆ ☆ ☆
  3501 New York Avenue, NE or 24th & R Streets, NE
  www.usna.usda.gov
- ☐ Kenilworth Aquatic Gardens ☆ ☆ ☆ ☆ ☆
  1550 Anacostia Avenue, NE
  www.nps.gov/keaq

Botanical Drawing

Find a plant species you like. Doodle it.

Plant name ______________________

Make your own soil & Garden

Do you have a compost bin at home? ○ Yes ○ No

What do you avoid putting in compost? Anything that:
○ Swam ○ Walked ○ Flew ○ All of the above

23% of all garbage can be composted. Compost:
○ Rinds ○ Fruit peels ○ Eggshells ○ All of the above

Clean up the yard! What can you put into the compost?
○ Weeds ○ Grass ○ Leaves ○ All of the above

What garden would you plant using your new soil?
○ Butterfly ○ Herb ○ Flower ○ Veggie

*The answer to all 3 questions above is **All of the above.***

My Fave Five plants

1.
2.
3.
4.
5.

Gardens

The Washington, D.C. area has lots of great gardens. We've only included ten here. Do a little research. How many more can you find? Were you inspired to plant a garden or trees?

■ Yes ■ No

The Great Outdoors

Washington, D.C. is not just a place to visit museums. Gardens and arboretums are not the only outdoor spots. Check off what you discover:

☐ **C&O Canal Towpath**

It is 184 1/2 miles of adventure. It begins in Georgetown and goes to Cumberland, Maryland

- ☐ Georgetown Canal Rides and Meet the Mules
- ☐ Canoe or rent a bike at Fletcher's, Jack's and Thompsons boathouses (D.C.)
- ☐ Hike at Great Falls on the Billy Goat Trail
- ☐ Visit Great Falls Tavern Visitors Center
- ☐ Get your Junior Ranger badge and find out more: www.nps.gov/choh/forkids/beajuniorranger.htm

☐ **George Washington Memorial Parkway**

This scenic road runs along the Potomac on both the Virginia and Maryland side.

- ☐ Ride the Carousel at Glen Echo Park, MD
- ☐ Visit the Clara Barton House, MD
- ☐ Sail at Belle Haven Marina, VA
- ☐ Visit Claude Moore Colonial Farm, VA
- ☐ Watch planes land at Gravelly Point, VA
- ☐ Ride, run or bike along the 18 mile long Mount Vernon Trail from Roosevelt Island to Mount Vernon, VA
- ☐ Take a hike on Roosevelt Island

☐ **Rock Creek Park,** a very large city park.

- ☐ Horseback ride at Rock Creek Park Horse Center
- ☐ Visit the Rock Creek Park Nature Center & Planetarium
- ☐ Join ranger lead programs ☐ Attend free summer camps
- ☐ Explore Pierce Mill & Dumbarton Oaks Park
- ☐ Bike or blade on Beach Drive Saturday and Sunday (Beach Dr closed to traffic - Broad Branch to Military Rd)
- ☐ Get your Junior Ranger badge and find out more: www.nps.gov/rocr/planyourvisit/index.htm

☐ **The National Mall**

- ☐ Ice skate at the National Gallery Sculpture Garden
- ☐ Ride, walk, jog or picnic on the National Mall
- ☐ Catch the cherry trees in bloom at the Tidal Basin

In D.C.'s Great Outdoors I would rather...

☐ canoe at Fletcher's **OR** ☐ kayak
☐ sail at Belle Haven Marina **OR** ☐ picnic
☐ jog the Tidal Basin **OR** ☐ stroll
☐ hike at Great Falls **OR** ☐ rock climb
☐ go fishing on the Potomac **OR** ☐ bird watch
☐ picnic at Hains Point **OR** ☐ play golf
☐ photograph the Mall **OR** ☐ doodle it
☐ Ride the carousel at Glen Echo **OR** ☐ at the Mall
☐ bike Rock Creek **OR** ☐ horseback ride
☐ ice skate at the Mall **OR** ☐ play frisbee
☐ do the paddleboats **OR** ☐ ride a canal barge
☐ ______________ **OR** ☐ ______________
☐ ______________ **OR** ☐ ______________

Poll your friends and family; what do they like?

GEORGETOWN

Founded in 1751, it is older than Washington, D.C. itself. What did you see?

- ☐ Old Stone House ☐ Washington Harbor
- ☐ C&O Canal ☐ Dunbarton Oaks
- ☐ Fave Shop ____________________
- ☐ Fave Restaurant ____________________

EASTERN MARKET ON CAPITOL HILL

At 7th and C St SE, visit this historic 1873 market. Weekends are best. Here you'll discover arts, crafts, and farm and flea markets. What treasures did you find at Eastern Market? __________

____

UNION STATION

This 1907 train station is one of the busiest spots in D.C. with over 32 million visitors per year. Take a historic tour. Catch it at Union Station:

- ☐ Old Town Trolley Tours and D.C. Ducks
- ☐ Open Top Sightseeing ☐ Tourmobile

OLD POST OFFICE

The second best view in D.C. Did you take the elevator to the tower?

OYes ONo

BEST EATS	FAVE SHOP	FUNNIEST SIGHT

FAVE 5 HISTORIC SPOTS

1.

ALEXANDRIA

Founded in 1749, it was George Washington's hometown. What did you see or do?

☐ Ramsay House Visitor Center ☐ King Street ☐ Torpedo Factory ☐ Masonic Temple ☐ River Cruises ☐ Ghost and Walking Tours ☐ Bike the Mount Vernon Trail

CHINATOWN AREA

Sights to see, things to do:

☐ Dim Sum at Tony Cheng's
☐ Chinese New Year's Festival
☐ Friendship Arch
☐ Spy Museum
☐ Verizon Center

☐ Science Museum ☐ National Building Museum
☐ American Art ☐ Portrait Gallery ☐ Ford's Theater

DUPONT CIRCLE-EMBASSY ROW

Located at the intersection of Massachusetts and Connecticut Avenues, NW. After the Civil War it was renamed after Rear Admiral Samuel Francis Du Pont.

☐ Chess game at the Circle ☐ Embassy Row
☐ National Geographic ☐ Phillips Collection
☐ Fondo Del Sol ☐ Bethune Council House
☐ Textile Museum ☐ Woodrow Wilson House

MY HOT SPOTS

What old town did you like best?
◯ Georgetown ◯ Alexandria ◯ Capitol Hill ◯ Chinatown

How many painted dragons did you count on Chinatown's Friendship Arch? ◯ 14 ◯ 82 ◯ 272

Did you take a C & O Canal Boat ride? ◯ Yes ◯ No

On Embassy Row how many embassies did you spot? ◯

What was your favorite part of the historic towns?
◯ Shopping ◯ Eating ◯ History

Answer: 272 painted dragons

HISTORIC HOT SPOTS

Shop, eat and people watch in a place where history was made. There are so many interesting spots and neighborhoods in Washington, D.C. Ask the locals what other spots they like, and what are their fave fun things to do.

If You Could...

take one modern invention back in time to the year 1800 what would it be... and why?

Your Space

This is your space. You make the rules! List your faves, doodle or daydream about what you'll eat for dinner tonight.

Who am I? I'm Benjamin Franklin, a founding father and a scientist. Can you find my statue outside the Old Post Office Pavilion?

At D.C.'s Historic Hot Spots I would rather...

☐ shop the shops **OR** ☐ hit the museums

☐ take the tourmobile **OR** ☐ walk the sights

☐ browse a book store **OR** ☐ a gift shop

☐ go to Eastern Market **OR** ☐ to Georgetown

☐ do a ghost tour **OR** ☐ a history tour

☐ play chess at Dupont **OR** ☐ walk Embassy Row

☐ take a river cruise **OR** ☐ hop on D.C. Ducks

☐ people watch **OR** ☐ window shop

☐ eat at a restaurant **OR** ☐ picnic in a park

☐ go to Union Station **OR** ☐ the Old Post Office

☐ ______________ **OR** ☐ ______________

☐ ______________ **OR** ☐ ______________

Poll your friends or family; what do they like best?

Top Ten Art Museums

Check off the museums as you visit them. Rate each.
Give them one star, five stars, or somewhere in between.

You are the Art Critic

What kind of art do you like?____________

☐ Modern ☐ Portraits ☐ Still Lifes ☐ Landscapes
☐ Photography ☐ Sculpture ☐ Folk ☐ Crafts
☐ Performance Art ☐ Conceptual Art
☐ Animation ☐ Commercial Art

On the National Mall

☐ National Gallery of Art ☆ ☆ ☆ ☆ ☆
A World of Art - United States' Art Collection
4th and Constitution Avenue NW - National Mall
www.nga.gov

☐ Hirshhorn Museum ☆ ☆ ☆ ☆ ☆
Walk "Around" and see Modern Art
7th Street and Independence Avenue SW - National Mall
www.hirshhorn.si.edu

☐ Freer and Sackler Galleries ☆ ☆ ☆ ☆ ☆
Asian Art in Two Museums by the Castle
Sackler:1050 Independence Avenue, SW - National Mall
Freer:Jefferson Drive at 12th Street, SW - National Mall
www.asia.si.edu

☐ National Museum of African Art ☆ ☆ ☆ ☆ ☆
An Underground Museum of African Art
950 Independence Avenue, SW - National Mall
www.nmafa.si.edu

Off the National Mall

☐ National Portrait Gallery ☆ ☆ ☆ ☆ ☆
See American History Through Portraiture
Eighth and F Streets, NW - Chinatown
www.npg.si.edu

☐ American Art Museum ☆ ☆ ☆ ☆ ☆
How Americans Create Art
Eighth and F Streets, NW - Chinatown
www.americanart.si.edu

☐ Museum of Women in the Arts ☆ ☆ ☆ ☆ ☆
Only Museum in the World Just for Women Artists
1600 21st Street, NW - Close to Dupont Circle
www.nmwa.org

☐ Phillips Collection ☆ ☆ ☆ ☆ ☆
The Modern Masters
1600 21st Street, NW - Close to Dupont Circle
www.phillipscollection.org

☐ Renwick Gallery ☆ ☆ ☆ ☆ ☆
An American Craft Gallery
Pennsylvania Avenue across from the White House
www.americanart.si.edu/renwick

☐ Corcoran Gallery of Art ☆ ☆ ☆ ☆ ☆
An Art Museum and College of Art
500 Seventeenth Street NW - West of the White House
www.corcoran.org

SKETCH IT

What are you inspired to sketch?

FAVE 5 WORKS OF ART

1.

2.

3.

4.

5.

WHAT KIND OF ARTIST WILL YOU BE?

Circle A, B, C or D. Which describes you best?

A. I like to arrange objects and colors.

B. I am unique and look at the world in my own way.

C. I love to get outdoors. I am at one with nature.

D. I am a people watcher. I am detailed and very focused.

MAYBE YOU WILL BE A...

Still Life Painter or Designer	If you chose A you could be a still life painter or a designer.
Modern Artist	If you chose B you may be a modern or abstract artist.
Landscape Artist	If you chose C you may be a landscape painter or maybe a nature photographer.
Portrait Artist	If you chose D you could be a portrait painter.

Blank Canvas

Your Space

Write your favorites, poll your friends! This is your space. You make the rules!

Tigers are one of the most endangered species in the world. Meet me at the National Zoo.

Your Space

Write about your day, your best friend or how you hate homework! You make the rules!

Cows are in the Bovidae family, which includes gazelles, antelope, buffaloes, and bison, as well as sheep and goats. Meet me at the National Zoo.

Your Space

Great job, you are at the end of the book. Sit back, relax, doodle or just take a nap!

Giant Pandas live in a small area in the mountains of China. They once lived in lowland areas, but now farming, forest clearing, and other human activities limit giant pandas to the mountains. Meet me at the zoo.

A Kid's Pocket Guide

All About Me in D.C.

Corkey Hay DeSimone has written and illustrated 27 children's books. She lives in Maryland, just minutes from Washington, D.C. Not a day goes by that she doesn't learn something new about our capital city.

Corkey got the idea for All About Me in D.C. while reading her Cherry Blossom Friends book at the Cherry Blossom Festival. Kids and families loved the fun facts so she decided to do a whole book filled with trivia, myths, polls and favorites.

The goal of this book is to empower kids and teens to become D.C. experts and to create their own D.C. experience.

Where were you inspired to go? E-mail us your fave facts, doodles, suggestions and photos of your trip(s) to D.C.

info@AllAboutMEinDC.com